The Lessons of Love and Life

AWAKENING TO SELF-LOVE AND HAPPINESS

JULIE KAY

BALBOA.
PRESS
A DIVISION OF HAY HOUSE

Balboa Press books may be ordered through booksellers or by contacting:

Balboa Press
A Division of Hay House
1663 Liberty Drive
Bloomington, IN 47403
www.balboapress.com.au
1 (877) 407-4847

Print information available on the last page.

ISBN: 978-1-5043-1232-5 (sc)
ISBN: 978-1-5043-1231-8 (e)

Balboa Press rev. date: 02/12/2018

I dedicate this book to the souls who strive to know and empower themselves. To the beings who acknowledge their divine right to live the lives of their dreams, and who find the courage deep within to make those dreams happen.

Contents

Thank You ix

Preface.. xi

Introduction xiii

Chapter 1   Getting off the Hamster Wheel................................. 1

Chapter 2   Soul Evolution and Destiny 12

Chapter 3   The Cross We Bear in Life Is Our Emotional Filter.......... 20

Chapter 4   Your Soul Lessons and Emotional Filters............................. 29

Chapter 5   Soul Lesson Combinations for All Soul Lesson Profiles... 67

Chapter 6   Unpacking and Reflecting....................................... 117

Chapter 7   The Consciously Connected Mind, Body, and Soul......... 144

Chapter 8   Consciously Connected Wisdom 162

Chapter 9   The Soul Lesson Gifts.. 180

Conclusion.. 189

Afterword.. 191

Special Offers.. 193

Author Bio... 195

Thank You

I wouldn't be able to do what I do, or to have learned what I've learned, without the support and some button pushing from many truly amazing people.

First, I would like to thank all of my soul teachers who have awakened me. This book could never have existed without your help. You taught me what can only be learned through experience.

To my beautiful children, Kirby, Darryl, and Jasmine, and to my grandchildren, Ryan and Dash. You remind me every day what unconditional love is all about.

My sincere gratitude also goes out to all of my many beautiful family and friends who have supported me and helped me not only with this book but in all areas of my business and life.

To Jesus. Although I don't practise religion, I feel the undeniable presence of love that comes from the sacred teachings of forgiveness, kindness, and compassion that illuminate from this master teacher, and I feel it guiding me in all that I do.

To my ever-so-patient guide and my mother who is in spirit. I am blessed to have this connection and to be able to hear and feel your guidance. Thank you. You have never let me down.

To the beautiful you who is reading this book: Thank you for inviting me into your life and having faith in my ability to help you set your heart free and shine from the inside out.

Preface

This book will help you delve deep into the deepest part of your being and uncover things that you may never have even noticed before. *The Lessons of Love and Life* will take you on an inner journey through a unique soul lesson and profiling system that will help you learn about your own emotional patterns and behaviour, as well as how they may be affecting and creating the very circumstances of which you are trying to rid your life.

Once you understand yourself from this much deeper level, and once you make conscious contact with what life is trying to make known to you every day, then through these teachings you will finally discover what has been holding you back for all these years and change it.

After two decades of helping people with spiritual profiling, I know that in order to move forward in life, we need to know and understand what is keeping us stuck. It's not quite as simple as thinking positive for the many who struggle with the underlying patterns and behaviours that keep sabotaging their results. *The Lessons of Love and Life* was written to help bring light to these underlying sabotaging patterns and lessons, as well as to guide you to self-understanding and accountability from this much deeper inner level.

This book is only for you if you are ready to laugh, cry, and face yourself head-on. You must be prepared to look at yourself and your life from a much deeper perspective, and you should be ready to own and change the part you play in creating your own happiness.

If you are ready to heal from the inside out, then *The Lessons of Love and Life* is the ultimate inside job to help you do it.

Introduction

My male client sat before me, arms crossed, and he told me straight up, "I am a sceptic. My wife came to see you, and I thought that you must have tricked her in some way, so I have come to see for myself."

In my mind, I thought, *All righty then. We'd better make this a good one!* In contrast to his hard demeanour, I could sense that this man held a lot of pain inside of him, and he was really very sensitive. I knew his manner was only a front, an invisible barrier he had placed around himself to protect his heart. Regardless of this knowing, he sat there looking intimidating and very uncomfortable.

I have been doing my spiritual work for over two decades now, and for the past twelve years as part of my full-time professional business. Therefore I have learnt not to take this kind of reaction personally; how he was feeling really had nothing to do with me.

When I tuned in for this man, the spirit of his deceased father came straight in and told me things there was no way I could have known, including all of the emotional turmoil my client was holding on to. Through his soul lessons, I helped him see how this was affecting his life today, and how his behaviour and interactions with others was being dictated by it.

This closed-off, stiff man sitting before me started to cry. He grabbed some tissues from the box on my table and apologised for sobbing. His body language changed, and he transformed into the person I knew was in there somewhere: his unguarded, sensitive self—someone he was desperately trying to hide and keep hidden from me and others.

Why do we hide our true selves? I am sure you, just like me, would prefer to come into contact with this man's true self instead of the defensive person he presented with. Wouldn't the world be a much better place if we could all show up without our emotional armour?

We show up like this because we are protecting ourselves from others and the perceived emotional threat they may cause us. This inadvertently disconnects us from others and our true and authentic selves. It's hard work to always keep yourself guarded, to show up how you perceive others want you to be, or to show up trying to be who you think you should be. It just too damned hard trying to keep everyone else happy, let alone yourself, isn't it?

But what is far worse than this is that in protecting ourselves, we can actually create the circumstances we are trying to protect ourselves from, through our own perceptions and behaviour. If you are repeating a pattern over and over again, then you are creating them, and it's time to understand how and why.

The reason you've been missing this is the same reason most people are missing it: because they don't know how to make conscious contact with their inner world and understand their own emotional lessons, filters, patterns, and behaviours. Therefore nothing changes, and these lessons keep showing up through life's issues, creating cycles of frustration, anxiety, fear, anger, and relationship problems.

There is a huge bonus to learning and doing this work. It will also make you more intuitive and connected to more than your eyes can see. However, this is not just about being intuitive; it's so much more than that. It will give you the ability to know and accept yourself, and it will help you find your true purpose in life so that you can follow your own pathway in the light of who you truly came here to be.

Are you ready? Awesome, let's learn more about what it really means to be you …

CHAPTER 1

Getting off the Hamster Wheel

You have bought the book. Thank you. Now what?

May I please make a suggestion? You start this inner journey right now by making a promise and a commitment to yourself that you will take some quality you time to read it. Even you triple-tasking supermums and workaholic budding entrepreneurs: I know you are quite capable of doing a million things at once, but seriously, this is all about you. So whether it's finding time to escape the rug rats, setting your partner up on a date with his PlayStation or her friends, or simply turning off your electronics, give yourself some you time so that you can make yourself and moving forward a priority in your life. Making yourself matter is the very first step in changing your life. Everyone else in your world will be much better off and will benefit from the happier person who comes out when you do so. I know you know this, but doing it for some people is a real challenge, and they are the ones who really need to read this book.

This book is about guiding you to making conscious contact with your inner world so that you can become internally guided rather than externally motivated. I want you to know you are already perfect, you are right where you are meant to be, and you have all the answers to your own direction deep within. The problem can be that you don't believe this, or you don't know how to connect to this inner part of you yet. Maybe it's both. This book is meant to guide you, and I hope you use it wisely. I urge you to trust your instinct over anything you read, hear, or learn from me or any other teacher. You are unique, you are creation itself, and all that you need to know and learn is already waiting for you to tap into it. This wisdom is simply to prompt and guide you to awaken this inner part of you, because that is where your purpose lies—and your purpose is only going to be truly right for you.

I wish I had a dollar for every time I have heard someone say, "If there is reincarnation, then I am never coming back here." Doing the spiritual work I do, I know there is more to our existence than this, and I've known it since I was a little girl. I can remember asking my mother, "Where was I before I was here?" She told me heaven. I replied, "But where is heaven then?" I was one of those kids who had to know everything. My poor mother couldn't answer me. And just as mothers do when we don't have the answers to those pesky questions, she told me to buzz off and play. But I knew, even as a little girl, that you can't *not* exist.

I have learnt over the years that we are eternal, and spirits do exist in another place. They do want to come back and have another go, because this existence has something the spirit world does not have: a physical body and physical things to play with.

I'm sorry to tell you this, but there are no jet skis or fancy cars on the other side; a spirit without a body has no need for them. Here on earth, however, we do have need for them, and you can also put your feet in the ocean, feel the sand between your toes, and feel the sun on your face. You can hold your child or fur baby in your arms, and you can make passionate, physical love to a partner.

We get pleasure from the physical world through touch and experience—something spirits can no longer do because they don't have physical bodies. So when I hear someone say, "I am never coming back here," I smile and think, *You may change your mind when you return to other side and no longer have the beautiful gifts the physical world has to offer.*

For you highly evolved souls who are thinking that we don't need the material stuff on the other side because we will have ascended out of the need for material things, I hear you. Yes, we will feel love on a much deeper level. But can you imagine what it would be like to just feel it but not be able to touch it, experience it, and play with it? To never wrap your arms around loved ones and hug them? To never feel what a physical hug feels like again? We already struggle with this here on the earth plane, when we lose loved ones.

When we pop our clogs and head over to the other side, we will experience an ascension into a realm that has other beautiful gifts, but not this body. I have still not chatted with a spirit from the other side that has appeared to me in a body. In my view, this existence on the earth plane holds a wonderful gift—the gift of the physical experience—and because we are here now, I feel we might as well make the most of it and enjoy it.

However, I do understand that with this human existence come some very real challenges that we can only experience in the physical world. These are the underlying causes and reasons some people have become so frustrated and hurt by life that they never want to come back. This is why I am passionate about sharing this wisdom: because we should all be loving and enjoying this physical experience, not loathing it so much that we never want to come back—or even worse, that we want to check out.

I have undergone many challenges in my own life, some of which I will share with you in this book. Like most of us here, life has felt like hell at one time or another. I am not perfect. I have made mistakes, I have hurt people, and I have been hurt, all of which has helped me to evolve and grow into the person I am today.

The essential word here is *evolve*, because that is what you are doing here. You are growing and learning to be you. If you don't evolve and keep moving forward by growing and learning, you become stagnant, and life becomes a challenge. Have you ever felt like you're stuck on the hamster wheel of life, and you want to jump off but can't? Let me ask you this: Are you stuck in a job you hate? Does your love life look more like a season from *Home and Away* or *Bridget Jones's Diary*? Do you have money, family, or health issues? Do you feel there is more to life than you are currently experiencing? If you answered yes to any of these—and hopefully not all of them—you have some evolving to do. If you did answer yes to all of them, that's okay. I've got you.

I've been on that hamster wheel, and it's crap. That's hell on earth right there. You go around and around in circles, doing and experiencing the same old, same old. If that's you, then it's time to get off the wheel because in case you haven't noticed, you're not a hamster.

As I've said, this is not a "think positively and you will be okay" or "just imagine it, and it will show up" kind of book. I am here to guide you in getting off the hamster wheel, and so there will be times that I am going to push your buttons. But I promise to do it with the utmost love in my heart. Before we get to the level of being able to keep our thoughts positive and magically attract all that we want into our lives, first we have to discover and uncover what is keeping us stuck.

I hope I can help stretch you out of your comfort zone. I need you to be out of your comfort zone because that means you have left the safety of your familiar patterns and are ready to evolve. By the time you get to the end of this book, you will love me and others for pushing your buttons. I promise that you will view button pushing in a whole new way.

Let me start off with a button-pushing statement right now: Stay with me. You will understand this on a much deeper level as we go along, and it will change your life. Life is not happening to you. It is happening because of you!

This is not a judgement to make you feel bad or guilty about yourself. It's a statement that is going to empower you. When you truly get this, you are ready to take control of your life by taking responsibility for everything in it, and therefore you'll drive your own evolvement. We are going to learn how the outside is a reflection of the inside.

In every moment, you are being shown what it is you need to change in order for you to grow and evolve and live the life you want. You are being shown this every day through all the connections in your life. Everyone you have an interaction with is a relationship in one form or another. *The Oxford English*

Dictionary defines a relationship as "the way in which two or more people or things are connected, or the state of being connected." On a higher level, we are all connected, and you make a connection with everyone you talk to or interact with on some level.

Your mother, father, sister, brother, daughter, or son, colleagues at work, the random girl at the checkout, and that pain in the bum on the bus—everyone around you is trying to show you what you are not getting, the stuff that is keeping you stuck. I will explain the how and why later.

Most of the time, we turn our attention to the outside, to the other person and the situation. You are now going to stop doing that, because if you're reading this book, you're ready to turn your attention within. Whenever we focus on what is happening to us through others and our situations, we are giving our power over to them. When you take responsibility and deal with it from an internal level first, you take back control, you find your solution, and you evolve out of it. Life will be full of happier moments because it will stop pushing your buttons.

To understand this, let me take you a bit deeper, and let's have a look at you and your split personality. Don't worry; we all have them. There are two sides to all of us that I liken to having a devil on one shoulder and an angel on the other. Both sides are driving us and telling us what to do. I will leave it to you to determine which side is driving you.

The Two Sides to Self—Understanding Our Dual Nature

Because we live in a world that contains physical things and we have physical bodies, we are governed by the law of duality. Duality means you can't have one side without the other. Everything that is physical in nature has two sides to it. Left and right, top and bottom—you can't have a front without a back. The law of duality shows up everywhere: good/bad, happy/ sad, problem/solution, day/night, young/old. It is the law of contrast and contradiction. Yin and yang symbolise this law, which tells us that two exact opposites make a whole. If you take this law deeper, it says that if you experience one side, the equal but opposite side must coexist, even if you are not seeing it.

If there is a problem, then there must be a solution. If there is a challenge, there must be a gift. If there is a loss, there must be a gain. How many times have you had something amazing happen that excited you to no end, only to have it followed by a complete downer? The law of duality must always be in balance. *Balance* is going to be a keyword throughout this book. If you have ever experienced inner peace, then you will know that it is not an excited, over-the-top feeling. It is a calm, almost-nothing feeling that feels balanced. If you are chasing that happy, excited feeling and are trying to keep it in your life, then you have some learning to do. You will come to understand that kind of excited will always be followed by experiencing a downer to an equal degree. That's why you see some people so over the top with their emotions one minute, and then really down the next. It's the emotional roller coaster effect.

Understanding yourself as a dual being is equally important. You have two very distinct sides to you, and together they make you who you are. Because you are here on the earth plane and are in a physical body, you are governed by this law while you are here. It will be impossible for you to simply experience only good emotions without the bad, because they are part of the same. These two sides that are dual in nature work in completely different ways. You have a yin side and a yang side.

The yang side is you as your physical body self. This side of the self is governed by the intellectual mind. It is the mind you think with, and you place your thoughts in this mind.

The intellectual mind thinks through beliefs and perceptions—in other words, how you see yourself and believe yourself to be, and how you perceive and believe others and their world to be. Those beliefs and perceptions have been formed over many years and culminate today as the knowledge you have learnt in total through your childhood and life experiences, education, and ancestral and cultural programming. This forms your ego. Childhood and ancestral programming are the beliefs you have learnt and taken on from your family and culture.

Simply put, your ego self with its learning, both good and bad, has formed your belief systems and how you now perceive you and your world to be. Your thoughts are filtered through all of this. As this ego side, you can only know what you know because it has been learnt through an experience, your education, or ancestral and cultural programming. If you haven't experienced or learnt it, or been programmed into it, then this side cannot know it.

If you go deeper than this, your ego and your life will reflect the soul lessons you have chosen to learn in this lifetime. More about that later.

This side of you has no intuitive ability at all, and it cannot see the future. It is more logic based. The way it evolves is through learning via experience or education, or by reprogramming. It can only perceive or analyse what an outcome will be, and it logically filters this through its own beliefs, perceptions, and experiences.

Here's an example of how this side figures things out. You have a problem, and so your mind gathers all its beliefs, experiences, and knowledge. It tries to analyse a perceived outcome by filtering your thoughts through all this information. Remember that this side has no intuitive value, and so it can only analyse and perceive what the outcome is likely to be. If it doesn't know the answer, it can do two things: (1) learn the answer through an experience, education, or advice, or (2) analyse and perceive what it thinks the answer will be based on what it has previously learnt and knows today.

Option two is where a lot of people get stuck. Because the intellectual mind has no intuitive value, it can sometimes procrastinate in overanalysing and trying to perceive an outcome. That outcome is often filtered through or compared to a past experience, and if that wasn't a good experience, it creates doubt and fear. If doubt and fear are present, this stresses the ego out even more, and it struggles to make a decision. If it does decide, the mind often goes into overanalysing that decision until you have thought yourself mad, and still you don't have an outcome. In other words, the thoughts keep going around and around in your head, but you aren't getting the right answer or an outcome. Sound familiar? You won't ever work it out in your head if you don't know. If you don't know, this side will have to learn it through education, experience, or advice.

When option two takes over, your life can be full of stress, anxiety, fear, doubt, and overthinking. That's the opposite of peace and happiness.

The physical yang, the ego side of self, is also where the comfort zone exists. For some people, the ego is more comfortable staying with what it knows or believes, even if that is not making them happy. The fear of the future, being unable to foresee an outcome, and the perceived fear of things not working out are ego traits that keep us stuck because the ego and the intellectual mind cannot see the future.

The good news is there is another side of you that can see the future.

The yin Side is you as your spirit side of self. This side is governed by the subconscious mind, which sits in the background of the intellectual mind. This mind is very hard to hear when the intellect takes over.

Have you ever had a thought randomly pop in your head? Where did it come from? You know you didn't logically think it, right? Then maybe a bit later, you discovered that what it said was right. Maybe it was something like, "Don't trust that person," but you did trust the person, who then let you down. Where did it come from? You didn't think it; it simply appeared. It will sound like your thoughts, but if you think about it, you didn't actually think it. It just randomly popped in. This is an intuitive thought. You will often remember these thoughts more on the occasions you didn't listen and thus learnt the hard way.

This side isn't governed by beliefs and perceptions; it is governed by a knowing. A knowing is often referred to as an inner voice, your intuition, and your gut instinct.

Have you ever had a knowing about something? You don't know how or why you knew it, but you simply did, and it turned out to be right. You may have felt something was going to happen, and it did. Or you had a feeling a friend was pregnant, and she was. This is the basis of gut instinct. There is no learning or analysis required; it simply felt right or wrong, and it was.

Your inner voice is what you hear popping into your mind. Gut instinct is based more on feeling, not emotion—that's different again. The inner voice is a deep, inner instinct within you that creates a knowing. When you learn to recognise this, it can help guide all the decisions in your life, especially those that your intellectual mind confuses.

You can start to practise this today. Instead of analysing a direction, feel it. Does it feel right? Does it inspire you and bring you a comfortable, peaceful feeling? If so, then it's a yes. If it doesn't, and it creates a deep, uncomfortable feeling or doesn't feel quite right, then it's a no. If you are confused, then you wait. You may need more information or the timing may not be right; sometimes it's both. Don't worry if you can't feel it yet. We have a lot more to cover to connect you to this side.

I have used this technique to determine my direction for many years. It has never let me down. You will also learn to have patience and sit with decisions when you don't know. It's the quicker way to get the outcome you want, even when patience is required. Believe me, it can save you from making rash decisions that take you off your path. Many people will make rash decisions because of fear of missing out. If it's meant to be, it will be. You will never miss out on something that is meant for you, but you can learn the hard way when it's not.

This part of you is eternal and connected to so much more than the eye can see. It is you when you are no longer housed in this physical body for this lifetime experience. I like to call this side of the self our soul guidance system. Just like a GPS, it can guide you through life, and this is who we are going to learn to make conscious contact with as we go along. This is the part of you that, when bought into balance, will consciously help you to take control and guide your life.

The law of duality says these two sides of self are part of the same, make up the whole, and are always in balance. If you are out of balance with one side, you will be out of balance in the other to the same degree. If you are out of balance on the yang side, then you may be too egotistical and logical, and you may become overanalytical, opinionated, critical, harsh, or unfeeling. You may become stuck in bad habits and negative thinking programs. This side can have a lack of confidence or an indifference to the spiritual and the creative. Your spirit self will be relegated to the background to an equal degree.

If you are out of balance on your yin side, you may be too airy-fairy and may be unable to commit to reality and get things done. You may try to be too saintly, giving and helping in detriment to yourself. You may be overly sensitive and suffer anxiety, guilt, and shame at not living up to your own or others' expectations and standards. When out of balance, this side can have a lack of confidence or an indifference to academic learning. The intellectual, logical yang side will be hidden in the background to the same degree. If you're out of balance, you can experience the negative from both sides to an equal degree, and you can flip between the two sides.

Bringing these two sides together and working in harmony with them brings balance to your life. We learn to use the yang, intellectual side for learning and planning, and the yin, intuitive side for making conscious contact and understanding and guiding our life's direction.

Everything on the yang, physical side of self is just for this lifetime, and because this side is all about learning, I believe this is the main reason we are having this lifetime experience. We are here to **learn.**

Emotions are also dual in nature. We have a opposite emotion for every emotion: happy/sad, fear/courage, angry/calm, shame/honour, guilty/ innocent, shy/confident, anxious/carefree. Therefore the emotions are either yin or yang. If your emotions are yang (sad, fearful, angry, ashamed, guilty, shy, or anxious), then they are being triggered by the physical, intellectual, ego side of self.

Depressed, defeated, and drained is a grade D in connecting to your spirit!

If your emotions are yin (happy, courageous, honoured, innocent, confident, or carefree), then you are making conscious contact with your spirit side of self, and you're more balanced.

Your emotions are a good signpost to gauge whether you are out of balance. The yang emotions are telling you that your intellectual ego side of self has something to learn in order to move forward. Makes sense, doesn't it?

Our Journey so far

You have promised to make yourself matter, by committing to making quality time to go through this book and look within. In other words, you have locked away all rugrats, partners, family, and electronics, right?

You allowed me to push your buttons by trusting that I will help you understand my statement "Life is not happening to you; it is happening because of you!"

We have determined that you have two distinct sides of self, and we have discussed how they coexist together but work very differently.

We have discovered that the emotions will help us gauge which side of the self is currently driving your life, and the yang emotions are telling you that you have something to learn.

Chapter 1 is just the beginning of you bringing your awareness to the inside by starting to witness which side of you is currently driving your life. In the next chapter, we are going to understand you as a conscious soul, and your place in a much bigger picture, so you can understand what you are really doing here.

CHAPTER 2

Soul Evolution and Destiny

> There is no logical way to the discovery of these laws,
> there is only the way of the intuition, which is helped by a
> feeling for order lying behind the appearance.
> —Albert Einstein

The bigger picture suggests that there is so much more going on than we can see in every given moment, and that everything is connected. When you grasp this bigger picture, you will understand that every thought, feeling, and deed is creating.

We are mini creators of our own reality, creating our own worlds by attracting what we are vibrationally sending out to us through the law of attraction. Everything in existence is linked in this bigger picture. Our own personal evolvement plays a part in the evolvement of those around us, which plays a part in the evolvement of the earth plane, which plays a part in the evolvement of the universe, which plays a part in the evolvement of all other levels of consciousness, which plays a part in the evolvement of the God consciousness! You play a very important part in something much bigger than you can imagine.

My knowledge of this comes from a deep sense of knowing from within. I see spirit and have since I was young. I know stuff and have no idea how I know it, but it simply comes. Science has yet to catch up to the metaphysical, and for centuries people like me just trust the wisdom that flows in and we keep moving forward, waiting for science to catch up. It is slowly, but there is still a lot to understand that is beyond our comprehension for this time in our evolution. I will try to give you my understanding, and if it resonates with you and creates and understanding of your own, great. If not, keep reading on because regardless of your beliefs, you will still understand the process of healing yourself and identifying what you are here to learn.

I know through spirit that there are many levels of consciousness. We on the earth plane are living in the physical consciousness, which encompasses all the planets in our solar system and beyond. The spirit realms don't contain physical matter; they vibrate at a higher vibration that is hard to see because, like air, it's invisible.

You can't see air, but if you take the air away, you will soon realise it exists. If you throw a bunch of leaves or a handful of sand into the wind, you can then see the direction the air is blowing for a split second. You have added matter to the air, and therefore you can now see it. It is the same for spirit. If you add matter via a physical body, you can see it. Simply because you can't see something, that doesn't mean it doesn't exist.

There is an invisible energy that keeps the planets turning, that turns a seed into a tree, that creates life, thoughts, and feelings. You can call this energy what you will: God consciousness, spirit, universe—it doesn't matter. It is a creative force that cannot be seen, but most people accept it exists.

The best comeback I have heard regarding believing this force exists was when I heard Dr. Wayne Dyer's response to a brain surgeon who stated that he had cut open many brains in his line of work but had yet to find a soul or spirit. Dr. Dyer replied, "Well, did you find any thoughts in there then?" Something invisible is driving all of this. I will leave you to call it what you wish. For this book, I will call it the God consciousness.

In early 2012, I watched a documentary called *The Thrive Project*. It was the missing link to my perception of how we coexist with these other realms, and how they are all connected yet distinctly individual.

I knew that the spirit realms were based on levels of vibration, and that the evolution of our souls depends on our own souls' vibration and the level to which we have evolved. I believe this theory of vibration is where religion gets its heaven and hell concept from—not that I believe in the traditional heaven and hell. I feel we are creating our own heaven or hell right here, and we are either evolving or not. I feel we can't rise to a level of vibration if we haven't evolved to it yet, but we can go down to a lower vibration. Your internal soul is an energy field that is always vibrating and always evolving, both here and in the spirit realm.

My light bulb moment came when I saw *The Thrive Project's* explanation of the energy pattern, called a torus. If you assume the soul or spirit forms this same vibrational energy pattern that is found on all levels of energy vibration, including atoms, the magnetic field around the earth plane, and our magnetic field or aura, then one could easily assume it is also the energy pattern of our soul. It even forms a channel at the top that we psychics have been banging on about forever. The flow of this energy pattern is magnetically drawing on the energy around it, and there is the law of attraction right there.

In quantum physics, Albert Einstein won a Nobel Prize for his discovery on pockets of energy wholeness called quantum pockets. These pockets of energy form a vibrational pattern out in the universe. This self-organising energy pattern draws on and uses its own surroundings to evolve, yet it is able to remain distinct within. These energy patterns are balanced and self-regulating, and they're always the same pattern no matter what their size. That's where the knowing within me really kicked in. Through the vibrational pattern of the torus, we are drawing everything that we need to evolve to us, using it to evolve. And yet we are able to remain a distinct spirit within, just as these giant quantum pockets of energy out in the universe are doing.

If you can now view your own spirit energy vibration as both a torus and a quantum pocket of energy vibration, then you can easily see how the law of attraction works by you attracting what you need to learn in order for you to evolve, yet you still remain a distinct individual spirit within.

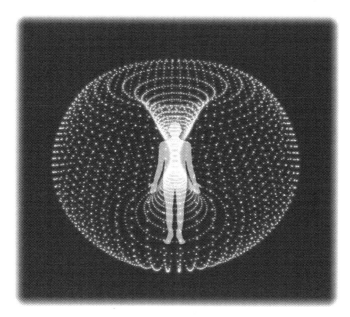

Based on this principle of energy flow, I explain the universe as everything existing within a massive quantum pocket of energy vibration, vibrating in the pattern of energy called the torus (we could call it God consciousness). Existing within this, and making up this pocket of energy vibration, are many other quantum pockets with different levels of energy vibration and consciousness. These form other planes of existence. Through the evolution process, each quantum pocket of consciousness is knowing and self-regulating itself, and through this process of self-regulation, they are evolving to a higher level of energy vibration and consciousness. Every quantum pocket of energy, right up to the God consciousness, is doing exactly the same thing, in exactly the same way, drawing on the energy around it and using it to evolve to a higher level of consciousness.

All energy vibration is constantly moving and aligning itself. If your soul moves to a higher consciousness, you become part of that consciousness and level. We are creating a consciousness of our own through our evolvement, which is connected to this much bigger picture.

Your soul vibration also contains conscious memory cells that hold all the information of every experience your soul has ever had thus far, including all experiences in all other lifetimes. The earth plane, in its mass consciousness, holds the memory cells of every energy vibration that it has ever experienced, including the lives of all who have existed on the earth plane. Every other realm of existence also has the memory cells of its experiences and evolution. You have left energy footprints wherever you have previously been—on the earth plane and the spirit planes—and you have the memory of these footprints stored in your energy cells and energy field. I call this your spiritual DNA. It is unique to you, and everything you are meant to learn while embodied here on the earth plane is already in your spirit. This is how it is possible to access past-life memories and psychic predictions.

You may be familiar with the universal law of attraction; it became popular when Rhonda Byrne released a film and book called *The Secret* in 2006. Rhonda contributed to a mass awakening of this universal law. A universal law is like gravity: it just is, and therefore it should be the same and work the same for everyone. After *The Secret*, a lot of people applied this law, and some people started to see the results. For a large number of people, it didn't work at all. Why is this? Why would it work for some but not for others? It's a universal law, and so it has to work the same for all! The answer is in your soul lessons and the underlying vibration they create within you. These soul lessons will determine what you are here to learn and experience right from birth. If you don't know these soul lessons exist, and you haven't learnt them yet, then you will be attracting them to you via your soul or ego energy vibration, which vibrates in the pattern of the torus. These soul lessons will be the basis of why your life is as it is right now and why you keep attracting and experiencing the same emotional patterns.

The conscious soul or ego, with its soul lessons, is like a magnet that is attracting and drawing to itself all that it needs in order to know itself and self-regulate to a higher level of consciousness. This vibration is contained in a physical body for this lifetime, and so the physical self will have the stronger vibrational pull, which means your physical side of self, through your intellectual mind, ego, beliefs, and perceptions, will be the basis of your attraction until you balance them with your spirit knowing. Have you ever heard the statement, "If you don't believe it, you won't achieve it"? You won't, and you won't attract it either. A belief is a deep, inner vibration you will create and draw to you. No amount of thinking will change this until you change the belief. We change a belief by learning and reprogramming, because this side is the learning side of self. I know I am repeating myself, but it is important to understand how it is all linked.

What you are most likely to attract is written in your spiritual DNA, which I call your soul lessons. What you need to learn in your current earth plane experience is being shown to you every day through your relationships. Remember this from earlier on? The good news is that if we are aware of this and know what it is we need to learn, we can work towards evolving it instead of living with the constant patterns of painful experiences that these lessons keep attracting and bringing to us.

It is vital you understand that the experiences you are having and the people in your life are a reflection of what you are attracting to yourself, so that you can learn about yourself in order to raise your consciousness level and evolve.

The way I get my head around this is by telling myself that every experience and every person in my life is my personal mirror, and what I see in them is a reflection of parts of me that I'm not able to otherwise see. This reflection will teach me what I need to know about myself so that I can evolve to a higher level of peace and happiness.

> Everything that irritates us about others can lead us to an understanding of ourselves. (Carl Jung)

I totally agree with Carl: this really does open up a can of worms for some people. However, when you view life in this way, it means you can no longer point the finger at others. You can no longer blame others for where you are in your life right now. It means that you are 100 per cent responsible for your life and your evolvement.

In every experience you have had in your life, there is one common denominator: you! The hardest part of growing and evolving in life is accepting your own part in it. You had no idea that you were subconsciously attracting and seeking out all the circumstances that could give you a shift in consciousness. If you only knew—but you didn't. No self-bashing or guilt allowed from here on in, okay?

Let me repeat: The experiences you are having, and everyone in your life, are a reflection of what you are attracting to yourself in order to learn about yourself so that you can raise your conscious level and evolve. You will know when you are faced with a lesson that can help you to evolve, because your emotional buttons will be pushed. There will be a negative emotional reaction that shows up from the yang side of the self. If people around you are pushing your buttons, they are reflecting a soul vibration that is within you that yearns to evolve and shift. If there was nothing there to shift or change, there wouldn't be a button that people could push, and you wouldn't have an emotional reaction or attract it in the first place. We don't like our buttons being pushed, and our first reaction is to point the finger at the ones doing the pushing. But if you point your finger at someone else, you will see that you have your other three fingers pointing back at yourself. Try it! Point your finger at something. See? Your thumb points to the sky, only one points at the other person, and three are pointing right back at you.

> If you are irritated by every rub, how will your mirror be
> polished? (Rumi)

Through the law of attraction, everyone whom you are attracted to or who shows up in your life is a vibrational match to what you are learning. They are also mutually learning what they need to learn and evolve. You wouldn't have been attracted to your partner or anyone in your life if you couldn't help each other learn something and mutually evolve. Yes, I know what you're thinking. Some don't get it, right? We all know people who haven't evolved and are still making the same choices and doing the same things they were doing at eighteen. Evolution is a conscious choice. You don't have to move forward, and if you look at the lives of these people who either don't know how or choose not to evolve, sadly their lives are usually full of ego, bitterness, resentment, and criticism. To them, it's always someone else's fault, and they become the victims of life.

However, you are evolving, and you are taking 100 per cent responsibility for your life, so all good, hey? (This is an Aussie term for, "You agree, right?" Although the New Zealanders will probably argue that it's theirs. It's a bit like Russell Crowe and Pavlova. We Aussies love claiming the kiwis' fame as our own.)

Let's do a review.

In this chapter, you discovered that you may be quite small in the big picture, but you play a pretty large role in the evolution of the universe. See? You are already part of something huge, but you would already know this deep inside. Most people have a feeling that they are here for a reason, and that's because they are!

You have learnt that we draw to us, like a magnet through our energy vibration, all that we need to learn and evolve. We know we are meant to be learning something when someone is able to push our buttons. Everyone in your life who is pushing your buttons is trying to help you see the part of you that you're ready to grow and evolve. Yes, we could wish they would shove off, but they don't, and if you do get rid of them, someone else will appear and take their place, and the emotional pattern will be repeated. When our buttons are pushed, it's time to look within.

What's up next? Well, be prepared for an aha moment. You are about to gain a much deeper understanding to how we not only attract but create what we want or don't want in life through our emotional filters, feelings, and behaviours.

CHAPTER 3

The Cross We Bear in Life Is Our Emotional Filter

> You stop attracting certain people and experiences, when
> you heal the part of you that no longer needs them.
> —Author Unknown

There is another aspect to the ego side of self that governs your ability to create peace and happiness, and this is your emotional filter.

The ego side of the self has created its own belief systems through the mind; I like to call these the big BS because they are usually full of a lot of self-defeating bullshit! A belief system is what the ego believes and perceives about itself and others. We know that not everyone believes and perceives things the same. Two people can have the exact same experience but see it completely differently. Who is right, and who is wrong? Neither. It's a perception that has been filtered through the emotional filters and egos of both parties. Because both parties have had different lives and experiences and have formed different filters and beliefs, it's impossible for them to perceive it in exactly the same way.

Wisdom Note. If you have ever tried to get another person to see your point of view, but they couldn't, and you ended up in a huge argument, you were wasting your time because they see it the way they perceive it, and unless they have your filter, they can't see it your way. You can go on and on about something all you like, but they are not going to get it. They can go have a learning experience, and maybe then they'll change their minds, but if it's not their perception or belief at the time, you are simply giving yourself heartburn. Knowing this can save a lot of arguments.

I also need to jump off topic and mention free will here. We all have free will; this is our own right to believe, perceive, and live as we choose. We are ultimately responsible for these choices either via attraction or karma. We don't have any right to try to change others or force our will on others, even if we feel we are helping them. Likewise, they don't have a right to do this to us. Children and the innocent (those who cannot look after themselves) are in our care, and we are here to guide and care for them until the age of eighteen, or until they no longer need caring for. Eighteen is spiritually the age of adulthood, where if we have guided them well, we should be handing over the responsibility to our kids to learn life for themselves. Again, we all know some forty-year olds who still haven't got this memo.

Nobody likes to be told what to do, and when you force or rescue people who haven't learnt their lesson yet, they will inadvertently revert to their original state because they haven't learnt it for themselves. Don't rescue your kids and others. Guide and help them to rescue themselves.

Let's get back to our emotional filters. We know we are attracting to us what we need to learn through the law of attraction. Now I want to take it deeper by helping you understand how we can then create an outcome through our emotional filter, which can have us repeating the emotional pattern and experiences until we learn and change them.

Your emotional filter has been set in childhood from birth to nine years of age by emotional events. Children are born innocent, intuitive, sensitive, creative, and full of love. Babies are more connected to their instincts and spirits. They have the instinct to cry when they are hungry, soiled, or scared. Babies see spirit, and I can give you hundreds of accounts where parents have witnessed this, because they haven't yet been programmed into the intellectual world of perception and beliefs. Their egos are only just being formed and aren't yet strong enough to direct their lives. As they settle into the earth plane, they start to take on the programming of the ego. As we learnt in chapter 1, the ego is formed through our childhood experiences, life experiences, education and learning, and the ancestral and cultural programming of the lives into which we are born.

The emotional events we experience as children can be minor (e.g., being reprimanded for naughty behaviour) or major (e.g., parents separating or abuse). But categorization is not relative. What we may consider as adults to be an insignificant event, in the eyes of a child who is innocent and sensitive, it can be very significant and emotionally charged. These emotional charges are what formed our egos' emotional filter.

It is in childhood that our ego learns early that we need to emotionally protect ourselves, and we learn to take control of our emotions to keep them in check. During an extremely emotional event, we do this by blocking our feelings and going into survival mode. We shut down emotionally and become numb—we don't feel anything. This is completely normal behaviour when dealing with any trauma. If we didn't do this, we wouldn't be able to cope. It's an inbuilt, natural coping mechanism.

When a child experiences an extremely emotional event—even something that might seem insignificant to an adult—he or she copes by shutting down and refusing to feel. This emotional shutdown is then added to over time as smaller, consistent emotional events continue to occur, which program and force the child to shut off and try to stop feeling. In other words, children learn to block out their pain. As parents and caregivers, we don't like to see our children upset, in pain, or angry. It's a natural response to want our children to feel better. Our children's pain can trigger our own emotional pain, and so we try to stop our children from feeling their pain; that way, we feel better too.

In doing this, we are unconsciously and unintentionally teaching our children not to feel and to block out their pain: "Don't cry. Nobody likes a crybaby." "Don't cry. Let's get you a lolly." "If you don't stop it, I will give you a smack." "There is nothing to be scared of. Now, stop getting out of bed." We are unconsciously training our children to block their feelings, which is their spirit side of self, and we're programming them more to the ego side of self. If you want your children to feel better, acknowledge their pain and tell them that you will hold them until it stops hurting, or tell them it's okay to be angry and frustrated, but we do it with responsibility and purpose; teach them to punch a pillow or something inanimate, not their siblings.

Every time a child shuts down or is shut down, a barrier is set up that shields the child from his or her own emotions and feelings, and the child becomes more and more sensitive to them. I would describe this as putting a layer of emotional concrete around the heart for emotional protection. The thickness of the layer depends on the emotional reaction that caused it. A heart can be blocked by lots of thin layers made up of many little emotional events, or by a few thicker layers made up of more traumatic emotional events.

The more layers of emotional concrete that we place around the heart, the more immune and hardened we become to ever wanting to feel these emotions again. The ego wants to protect itself from feeling the emotional reaction and hurt again. We don't like feeling pain or negative emotions because they trigger the emotional pattern that set them up in the first place, as well as all the experiences that have added to them along the way, making the ego very sensitive to the emotions and on guard to any experience it perceives will repeat these emotional reactions and negative feelings.

That's what it thinks, anyway. It is the opposite that actually happens—it can end up creating the emotional experience from which it is trying to protect itself.

Remember the intellectual mind cannot see the future; it can only filter thoughts through what it knows today. If that filter is full of emotional turmoil, then your ego is not only going to try and block you from feeling these past feelings and emotional reactions, but it is also very sensitive and on guard to how you perceive and believe an experience to be, which can affect the way you react and respond to it. You will be filtering your perceptions through your emotional filter, and if that is out of balance and in reaction to soul lessons, then you will create the very thing from which your ego is trying to protect you.

Let's use a couple of examples to explain this further.

Someone has the lesson of independence with the lesson of abandonment, and her experience was emotional abandonment as a child. This person is now very sensitive to the feelings of abandonment. Her ego will be on guard to any experience or situation that could result in abandonment, and her ego will try to protect her from it. In this energy of trying to protect herself from feeling abandoned, she will perceive all situations through this filter and act accordingly. This may result in her constantly relying on or leaning on others for reassurance that she is loved and wanted, even using drama as way to gain this evidence through attention. She may become very needy as she constantly wants reassurance that she is not going to be abandoned. Others may feel this is too much pressure and want to move away from her, which then creates the abandonment she feared in the first place. On the dual side, she may be very demanding or opinionated and push against others with her values as a way to emotionally protect herself through a hard exterior. She may also keep emotionally detached from others, and this shuts others out and pushes them away, in the end creating the abandonment she feared.

Another person may have the lesson of trust with the lesson of belief. He may have had his trust knocked as a child, or maybe he wasn't believed. His emotional filter will be very sensitive to this, and his ego will be on guard towards trusting or believing in others or himself. If he doesn't trust others, his ego could be constantly searching for the evidence of other people's motives or untrusting behaviours—checking up on them, accusing them, and overquestioning them. The other people are dammed if they do and dammed if they don't, and so they often end up either doing the behaviour they are accused of or lying to save themselves from the constant grilling, creating the trust issue this person feared. If this person doesn't believe he is capable of something, he won't allow himself to get past it. What you believe, you achieve—if you don't think you can, you won't. Therefore he will be creating his own lack of belief as a reality.

If your ego is presenting through your emotional filter, and you are struggling with yourself through and around others, then your ego is causing you pain. The pain comes from your own perceived potential threats to your ego's emotional well-being. The way you view yourself or the way you feel others view you can cause an emotional reaction that triggers your soul lessons, your emotional filter, and limited beliefs habits, which in turn affect your perception of a situation and your behaviour, which can lead to you creating the event your ego feared and was trying to protect you from.

Is my statement now starting to make sense? Life is not happening to you—it is happening because of you!

Why? Because …

1. You are drawing to you, through the law of attraction, what you have chosen to learn and evolve in this lifetime.
2. You create what you have not yet learnt through your own ego reactions and behaviour.

I know some of you will still have doubts and may even be yelling at me right now, saying, "I never asked for [insert your argument here] to happen to me."

Stay with me. I haven't explained the soul lessons yet, and we still have deeper to go.

The examples I have just used are very simple; I used only two soul lessons. There are forty-four combinations of soul lessons, all creating different emotional filters and ways of perceiving; more about them in the next chapter. These filters are often quite hidden from us—if they weren't, we would all be emotionally fulfilled, happy, and kissing rainbows.

Wisdom Note. I just want to add a note on what I believe about destiny. I believe we have a destiny, but there are many different pathways to it, which are all linked. I believe that you will fulfil your destiny based on your free will and the choices you ultimately make. We know a lot of people die with their music still in them because they have not been able to overcome the ego's programming of belief systems and emotional filters. Don't let this be you.

Time for a review—and a stiff drink if you need one.

Every emotional experience you have had in your life has created your emotional filter, through which that you now perceive your present life.

This governs your behaviour, which can create the outcome the ego fears and is trying to avoid as your own reality.

Deep, isn't it? This is what going within is all about.

In the next chapter, I am going to help you identify your soul lessons and your emotional filter. You can't change something you are not aware of; if anything you have read so far is bringing up any form of self-criticism, consider this a virtual slap. Stop it! That's your ego, and it doesn't know what it doesn't know because you haven't learnt it yet!

I love that I no longer have to wear a mask.
By Sue Kenny

Even though I felt the love of spirit guiding me, I chose to block out most of my connection to my spirit guidance for a turbulent thirteen-year period of my adult life. I always wondered why I was so different than other people and why I did not fit in.

Reflecting now, I can see that I was playing the part of a victim, blaming others for my lack of happiness, joy, respect, honesty, self-worth, and love in my life. I did not take responsibility for my part in what was happening. I was drama filled and on high alert twenty-four seven. I believed I had to change and save the other person before I could save my children and myself. I lived in the past whilst dreaming of a better future.

On 23 March 2009, I was finally ready to wake up and start my soul-healing journey. A Heal Your Life workshop started the journey, and then I studied and implemented the Four Agreements into my life.

My soul was yearning, ready, and searching for deep soul healing. The universe presented Julie Kay to guide me towards my greatest tools for the next part of my healing journey.

Julie's book *Soul Lessons to Soul Mate* was a life changing moment. I experienced so many aha and soul understanding moments about my life. It was as if a dark veil had been lifted, and every decision, situation, and reason for my life was starting to make sense to me. I loved Julie's straightforward, matter-of-fact way of delivering guidance and strategies for my soul lessons.

I loved knowing and understanding my soul lessons, and attending the Love Life Retreat was an amazing experience. I now had soul tools and strategies to heal my ego and assist me to make decisions in my life that are for my highest good. I finally began taking responsibility for my life again. I felt empowered, energised, empathic, enlightened, forgiving, authentic, and loving towards myself and everyone around me.

Now I use the tools, strategies, and knowledge of my soul lessons in every moment. I am constantly checking in on my soul reactions and feelings about every situation. This enables me to acknowledge, feel, and move through situations quicker and easier.

I now have strong, healthy boundaries in all aspects of my life. I say no without feeling I need to explain or feel guilty. I know that I am love and lovable. I am accepting and acknowledge everyone has his or her own journey, which is different to mine. I don't have to help or control anyone else's journey. I live in the moment; I don't dwell in the past or the future for long periods of time. I love and accept all parts of myself. I am the only one who is responsible for the amount of happiness and love in my life.

I am loving life again, and I love not having to wear a mask and be what everyone expects me to be. I love living life as the authentic, strong, intuitive, loving person I now know I am.

CHAPTER 4

Your Soul Lessons and Emotional Filters

> God allows us to experience the low points of life in
> order to teach us lessons we could not learn in any other
> way. The way we learn those lessons is not to deny the
> feelings but to find the meanings underlying them.
> —Stanley Lindquist

In the fifth century, the Greek mathematician Pythagoras founded geometry and presented the theory that everything is mathematical in nature. Pythagoras also taught that the human soul was immortal, and he spoke of cycles, patterns, and the influence of universal laws on the soul. He taught that numbers were the essence of all things, including our personality and destiny. Pythagoras is also considered to be one of the founders of numerology, although its origins have been found to date back to as early as the twentieth century BC in Hindu scriptures known as Vedas.

You may be aware of numerology and may even have used it in the past to determine your life path, personal year, and personality numbers. I have used numerology for over two decades now, most of which has been via spiritual profiling, and I have discovered that this discipline can provide very specific lessons not only for the life path but also for our emotional filters and relationships.

For profiling lessons, numerology focuses on what we call the life path number or destiny number. This is the date of your birth added together to get to a single number. You can buy any numerology book or use sites on the

Internet to discover what your number means and what your life lessons are. My formula, however, focuses on specific soul lessons, combinations, and filters. We still use the life path formula, but we don't reduce it to a single digit as numerology has you do. Just as important are the other numbers that make up the total number. Through many years of emotionally profiling people with the numbers, I discovered very unique patterns appearing, and spiritual profiling was born. These lessons have helped thousands of people accurately understand their emotional lives on a much deeper level, and they have truly stood the test of time.

These soul lessons are what we are learning, and we learn them through our relationships with others. The soul lessons will play out through all the relationships in your life. If someone is causing you to experience any kind of emotional reaction within you, then that person is pushing your soul lesson buttons.

It's time to help you work out your own soul lessons and the emotional filters they create. By using your destiny or life path numbers with my formula, you will discover what your ego has been trying to protect you from. I call this your soul lessons relationship blueprint and profile. It will depend on you (as an individual) and your childhood experiences as to the extent these lessons will affect your life. Reactions to lessons can materialize in a range of experiences, from painful and destructive to those that are experiencing a little bit of disharmony; this is determined by you and the sensitivity to your emotional filter.

Your Soul Lesson Relationship Blueprint and Profile

Here's how to determine your relationship blueprint and profile using the basic numerology life path or destiny number calculation.

Add all numbers in your birth date. For example, if your birthday were July 10, 1974, (07/10/1974), you would add $0 + 7 + 1 + 0 + 1 + 9 + 7 + 4$. That equals 29, so reduce it further: $2 + 9 = 11$, and $1 + 1 = 2$

In the space provided on the next page, write down this number and then keep adding and recording these numbers until you get to a single number:

Your relationship blueprint and profile numbers are all the numbers from the total of your date of birth down to the single digit. The single digit number is the master lesson. The other numbers are considered equal lessons. In our example (29 = 11 = 2) the relationship lessons are 2, 9, 1, 1, and 2, with the last 2 being the master lesson and the other numbers being equal lessons.

The following list shows the specific relationship lessons associated with each number. Write down the corresponding lessons relating to your own blueprint and profile numbers next to them.

1. Independence: the lesson of abandonment
2. Codependence: the lesson of attention
3. Self-worth: the lesson of acceptance
4. Stability: the lesson of support
5. Control: the lesson of freedom
6. Commitment: the lesson of sharing
7. Trust: the lesson of belief
8. Security: the lesson of achievement
9. Humility: the lesson of giving and receiving
10. Repeated (from a previous life) and not yet completed

Special Note: If you have a 1 or a 2 as a soul lesson in your profile, then you automatically have the other. 1 and 2 soul lessons go hand in hand—you can't have one without the other, even if only one is present. The reason for this is that these two lessons are dual in nature: independence/codependence, abandonment/attention. From this point, they will be placed together for this reason.

Our example of 07/10/1974 equals the relationship lessons 29/11/2.

> 2 = Codependence: the lesson of attention
> 9 = Humility: the lesson of giving and receiving
> 1 = Independence: the lesson of abandonment
> 1 = Independence: the lesson of abandonment
> 2 = Codependence: the lesson of attention

Another example would be 12/04/1994 = relationship lessons 30/3.

      3 = Self-worth: the lesson of acceptance
      0 = Repeated, not completed
      3 = Self-worth: the lesson of acceptance

Use the provided space to determine your own relationship blueprint and profile.

_____

_____

_____

_____

_____

_____

These lessons run in order, with the master lesson being the last single digit. All of these lessons will intertwine and play out through each other, forming your specific emotional filter. Generally, it will be after you understand the first numbers that you will finally be able to discover and integrate the master lesson. This doesn't mean the master lesson will be left to the last minute; it can still show up at different times throughout the relationship lessons, with the full understanding of this lesson coming after that.

The person in our first example has five relationship lessons (2, 9, 1, 1, 2) to learn in this lifetime. The fact that the number 1 appears twice simply amplifies the vibration of this lesson. The double 2, with the second 2 being the master number, also amplifies this lesson. It also means that this lesson will be the hardest of the lessons.

The person in our second example (3, 0, 3) has only two lessons, and they are both the number 3. Again, the double 3 amplifies the energy of this lesson, which has to do with self-worth, the lesson of acceptance. There are no other lessons involved in this person's profile, and so the relationship lessons are all based around the lesson of self-worth. The 0 in this person's relationship blueprint and profile means he or she is repeating this lesson from a previous lifetime, which also can often mean a heightened sensitivity to the emotional lesson of self-worth and acceptance.

Approximately 95 per cent of relationship blueprints in my collection of thousands of profiles—especially for anyone born prior to the year 2000—contain a 1, 2, or 3. These three lessons are very specific lessons relating to our sense of self. It is absolutely no coincidence that there are a lot of people who struggle with their personal power and self-worth in their relationships or have co-dependency issues.

The Evidence and Experiences of Your Soul Lessons

In chapter 3, we learnt that our soul lessons emotional filters were set up between the age of zero and nine years of age. This is through an emotional experience or experiences that caused an emotional shutdown. The emotional filter will be your soul lesson teaching; it is what you have chosen to experience emotionally and overcome in this lifetime.

Now that you have discovered what your lessons are, it's time to compare them with the next module. In this section, the statements are used to prompt your memories so that you can identify how they have been set up for you in your childhood and how they may have been showing up in your relationships with others. Use only your specific soul lesson numbers and leave the rest. All your lessons will influence your relationship experiences, so you must view all your numbers even if you can relate more to one particular number than another.

As an emotional experience, we can feel all the nine lessons in each and every one of us. You may read another that sounds like you, however the emotional filter that your soul lesson combination creates will be the deep work that you may be missing. Through the many years of soul lesson profiling I have learnt that the perceived pattern can show up in different ways, but the person's lessons are always there as the underlying, deep emotional block. If you find you are coming up with other lessons, feelings, and emotions, then it's usually because you haven't gone deep enough.

Some numbers will contain the same statements as other numbers because the same experience can set up different emotional reactions and filters. For example, sexual, physical, or emotional abuse all addressed under 1,

3, 5, and 7. These lessons show the different emotional reactions with which a person must deal. The #1 profile reacts with abandonment issues because they relate to feelings of being neglected. The #3 profile reacts with self-worth and confidence issues because they relate to feelings of worthlessness. The #5 profile addresses control issues because they relate to feelings of powerlessness. The #7 profile relates to trust issues and difficulty in trusting again. One experience can set up different emotional filters, and it's the vibration of the lesson that determines the emotional filter and reaction pattern.

It is also very important to remember the law of duality. As already mentioned, the lesson of the 1 and 2 are dual in nature, and so those two lessons show you the duality. All the other soul lesson numbers also contain a duality. Every lesson contains exact opposites, and there is variance in the severity or intensity of every lesson. For example, lesson 5 addresses control; it is the lesson of freedom. The variance of control refers to emotional experiences of severe control to mild control. The duality of this lesson is learnt through the opposite, which ranges from being controlling to having no control. There is variance and duality in the experience of every lesson.

Exercise

For this exercise, I have provided information about each soul lesson, as well as a checklist of related experiences that you might have had. For each lesson you have written down (from your numerology calculations), tick off the statements that relate to your experiences. When you have completed all the lessons, allow your mind to wander over the past and identify the experiences and the emotional patterns that relate to your lesson and statements. The first step in learning a lesson so that you can release it is to understand its origin and its effects.

If a statement is the exact opposite to your actual experience, then write it out. You have just discovered the duality of your lesson. Remember that every lesson can have a variation in its intensity or duality.

1. Independence: the lesson of abandonment

The lesson of abandonment attracts situations and experiences that leave a person feeling emotionally disconnected from others and alone in life.

If you are learning the lesson of independence, you may find that you attract situations that call on you to be comfortable with being yourself, standing up for yourself, and exhibiting healthy independence. The duality of this lesson is that you may need to bring your independence into balance if you are too outspoken or don't allow others to help you or connect to you emotionally, because you are holding them away.

2. Codependence: the lesson of attention

If you are learning codependence, you may find that you attract situations that centre on and around codependence. Either you are codependent, or you attract codependent people. You can often place too much attention on the needs of others, rather than your own needs, as a way to feel good inside.

You may find that you have unrealistic intense feelings of wanting something or someone to fulfil you. You may need to feel or hear often that you are loved, and you want to experience constant contact or reassurance from your partner and others. When you are alone, you crave emotional attention or contact with others. The duality of this lesson is attracting relationships in which you keep yourself emotionally distant for fear of getting hurt. Codependants may also want to fix, or feel responsible for changing, another's life for the better, rather than focusing on themselves and their own happiness and allowing others the responsibility to learn their own way.

Your soul lessons are set up in childhood. Tick off the statements that reflect your childhood experiences.

	You were born into a family in which a parent either left, died, or wasn't around due to other commitments.
	You are adopted.

	Your parents experienced an addiction (e.g., sex, alcohol, drugs, gambling).
	You have a disability.
	You are an only child and felt lonely in childhood.
	You found it difficult to fit in as a child.
	You experienced many situations of rejection.
	You are the eldest in the family and had to be responsible for or be a role model for younger siblings.
	You are the youngest in the family and had no responsibility.
	Your parents were strict and didn't allow you to be independent.
	Your parents weren't able to show you emotional support and responded to your issues by ignoring them or reflecting them back to you (e.g., by saying, "You will be fine").
	You felt you had to be a high achiever.
	You were a bossy or outspoken child.
	You were bullied or you bullied others.
	You were a very shy and sensitive child who never stood up for yourself for fear of reaction.
	Your parents were not able to show you they cared by showing you emotional support, giving hugs, or including you as a special part of their lives.
	You felt emotionally let down as a child.
	You were born into a large family in which your parents had little time to share their emotions, or you perceived they had favourites.
	Your parents didn't take much interest in your social activities and never went to watch your sports games or your school activities.

	Your parents had an emotionally rocky marriage or were separated.
	You were a shy, sensitive, or clingy child.
	You used negative behaviour as a child to get attention.
	You were not taught responsibility as a child, or feel you were given too much responsibility and lost your childhood.
	You were spoilt as a child.
	You were left with a lot of carers or babysitters.
	Your family did not have a lot of money, and you missed out on a lot as a child or were rejected by others because of this.
	You were not made to face the consequences of your choices.

This lesson may have attracted you to certain relationship and life experiences. Tick the statements that reflect yours.

	Others have rejected your values, goals, and dreams.
	You attract people, or you are a person with an addictive personality (e.g., gambling, eating disorders, emotional eating, drugs, alcohol, pornography, compulsive lying, sex, extra-relationship affairs).
	You avoid relationships or emotional connection to others for fear of getting hurt.
	You believe you're very different and that others don't understand you.
	You prefer to hang out with much older or much younger people.
	You find you attract very opinionated people who try to tell you what to do or want to change you or vice versa.
	When you're around others or in a relationship, you miss your independence; when you're not, you are lonely.
	You attract strong-willed people, which creates lots of arguing.
	You are quite serious in life and lack spontaneity and fun.

	You attract partners who always want their own way, challenge you, and don't show you their emotions.
	You have been telling yourself and others that you are happy being on your own, yet you feel quite lonely.
	You attract relationships and people who end up abandoning you, and you have no idea why.
	You are very needy and want emotional support from others, or you attract others who need you to emotionally support them.
	You have attracted partners who are emotionally distant.
	You find it hard to be decisive and make decisions.
	You attract people and partners who do the opposite to what they expect of you; for example, your partner states that you must save rather than spend money, and then he or she spends money on something he or she wants.
	You don't have the courage to follow your own direction and will do anything to keep the peace, even when it's a detriment to you.
	You feel like you are always mothering or caring for others.
	You spend too much time planning, analysing, reliving your experiences, or planning on how your next interaction will go and what you are going to say.
	You use alcohol or drugs to gain courage or to feel better.
	You or your partner have an overactive sex drive that associates sex with love.
	You wear your heart on your sleeve and rush into new friendships and relationships that end up letting you down.
	You have experienced a lot of failed relationships.
	You are emotionally needy and insecure in relationships.
	You have experienced constant ups and downs, and there always seems to be drama in your life.

| | You suffer from anxiety and worry about what other people think of you. |
| | You over help others and don't know how to say no. |

The Feelings of Independence and Abandonment

If you have the independence lesson with the lesson of abandonment, this soul lesson will leave you feeling abandoned, disempowered, unheard, invisible, rejected, isolated, restricted, hardened, opinionated, superior, or ignored.

The Lesson of Independence and Abandonment

Your lesson is to be aware that when you abandon yourself, others will abandon you too!

If you are learning the lesson of independence and abandonment, it's important to:

+ Focus on becoming comfortable with your own values, visions, and goals. Never put to the side your own values and dreams just to fit in.
+ Learn to love and accept yourself for who and where you are, and accept others for who and where they are.
+ Learn to integrate fun into your life and not take everything so seriously.
+ Learn to connect to people on an emotional level. People who are experiencing this soul lesson are natural leaders, and they can either exhibit this by being bossy or not exhibit this by allowing others to boss them.
+ Learn to give unconditionally and consider others without judgement.
+ Learn to respond to criticism rather than to react to it, and to discuss any issues that arise with confidence and diplomacy.

+ Learn that it is okay to be vulnerable and that it is not a sign of weakness. This will allow you to accept help from others and to connect to them emotionally.
+ Learn to stand in your power at the appropriate times in a responding nature rather than a reactive one.

The Feelings of Codependence and Attention

If you have the codependence lesson with the lesson of attention, this soul lesson will leave you feeling insecure, unloved, disadvantaged, needy, detested, neglected, deprived, insignificant, or indecisive.

The Lesson of Codependence and Attention

Your lesson is to understand that when you give loving attention to yourself, others will then give loving attention to you.

If you are learning the lesson of codependence and attention, it is important to:

+ Focus on the awesomeness of you and build yourself value. Learn to say no and to stop doing things or giving out of obligation.
+ Understand your own feelings and emotions by giving yourself self-love and attention.
+ Look at your emotional health and work on any self-defeating habits or addictions.
+ Accept and honour yourself for who you are and where you are right now. Become aware of times when you are trying to gain attention to feel better about yourself or a relationship.
+ Take relationships very slowly and get to know your partner. You may even need to abstain from sex while you get to know a partner, because the codependent will often associate sex with love and find it difficult to hold back his or her emotions. This will help you to keep your rose-coloured glasses at bay and allow you to see a relationship for what it truly is.
+ Understand your feelings of longing. The codependent person is one that suffers from the constant feeling of longing. This longing

is a needy feeling that is looking for fulfilment outside of the self. This is codependency! This kind of longing to be connected and nurtured cannot be fulfilled for long periods of time using people, objects, or experiences.

3. Self-worth: The Lesson of Acceptance

The lesson of acceptance attracts situations and experiences that leave a person struggling with self-esteem and confidence, and it forces a search for proof of his or her worthiness through the acceptance of others. This soul lesson is also teaching a deep inner acceptance of oneself.

If you are learning the issue of confidence and self-worth, you may attract situations that knock your confidence. You may have attracted experiences of rejection and constant letdown, and your experiences have left you feeling that you are never good enough. The duality of this number brings to your awareness the possibility that you are using others to build your self-esteem by treating them badly. Do you reject others, put them down, or say hurtful things? Whenever we treat someone badly, it is usually because we are trying to feel better about ourselves.

Your soul lesson is set up in childhood. Tick off the statements that reflect your childhood experiences.

	You were a very shy and sensitive child and experienced many situations that your sensitive soul took personally.
	You had parents who left, died, weren't around, or didn't want anything to do with your upbringing.
	Your parents were emotionally unresponsive to your needs.
	You have experienced sexual, physical, or verbal abuse.
	You were teased or bullied.
	You struggled academically or with sporting activities.
	You were put down as a child by a parent, teacher, or other significant person in your life.

	You were told children should be seen and not heard.
	Your parents were very strict, and you felt as if you could never do the right thing.
	You rarely received positive feedback for anything you did; there was mostly criticism or a push to do better.
	You were brought up by your grandparents or placed in foster care.
	You felt left out or picked on by other family members.
	You lived a very sheltered childhood, and your parents were always trying to keep you safe by telling you what to do.
	Your parents bought you up with a pessimistic view of others and the world.
	You never wanted to, weren't allowed to, or weren't encouraged to try different experiences as a child (e.g., a sport or something creative).
	You were taught to feel ashamed or guilty for behaviours you innocently did in your life.
	Your where teased and made to feel ashamed of yourself.
	You felt rejected by others.

This lesson may have attracted you to certain relationship and life experiences. Tick the statements that reflect yours.

	You are the victim of sexual, mental, or verbal abuse.
	You have had partners who continuously look at, admire, or flirt with others.
	You experience situations of rejection or often feel rejected or left out.
	You have had experiences with others who have undermined your self-confidence and left you feeling as if nothing you do is ever good enough.

	A partner had an affair, left you, or wouldn't commit to you—or you have done this to a partner.
	You feel that you are neglected by loved ones who place more emphasis on everyone or everything else.
	You seek out reassurance and acceptance and need constant reassurance from others that what you do is good enough.
	You judge yourself harshly, by blaming yourself and looking for what's wrong with you or what you've done wrong. You feel that everyone else does too.
	You have attracted partners with addictions (e.g., porn, sex, alcohol, drugs, gambling), and they blamed their addictions on you.
	You have attracted players—people who are in a relationship for only short-term gain.
	You have tried to mother your partner or feel as if your partner sees you as a mother figure.
	You have seen yourself as a father figure to your partner or feel your partner wanted you to be a father figure.
	You have attracted pessimistic people who focused on everything that was negative and wrong and who loved to tell you your faults.
	You have attracted a partner who didn't support your beliefs, talents, work, or direction and wanted you to change.
	You feel as if you always need to justify yourself and explain yourself.
	You attract lazy and self-centred people who don't end up caring about you.
	You suffer from anxiety and feel like everyone is judging you.

The Feelings

If you have the lesson of self-worth with the lesson of acceptance, it can leave you feeling not good enough, insecure, worthless, shamed, self-doubting, rejected, critical, judgemental, cynical, or disgraced.

The Lesson

If you have this lesson, you must understand that when you find self-acceptance and self-love, others will accept and love you for who you are too.

If you are learning the lesson of self-worth and acceptance, it is important to:

- Work on your confidence, build your courage, and don't take others and life so sensitively or personally.
- Stop using the opinions of others as a measure of your self-worth. Instead, build your strength and confidence from within.
- Work on your self-acceptance and self-love.
- Keep it real, and don't try to perceive what others may be thinking or saying about you. Most of the time, your assumptions will be incorrect and based on your own limiting beliefs about self. My motto is what everyone else thinks about you is none of your business, because what you think matters so much more!
- Practice self-help, education, and positive reprogramming, all of which work in changing your limiting self-belief system, which will result in a more confident and self-believing you.
- Work through issues of abuse of any kind with a counsellor or healer to recover your self-worth and confidence.

This is the most common individual lesson, and it appears in approximately 65 percent of profiles prior to the year 2000. I believe it's also one of the hardest to heal for most people. It will take consistent effort to reprogram your self-worth, but it can be done. Learning not to take everything so personally and having a much broader understanding of human nature will help you do this. The gift of the #3 profile is communication and counselling, and both these skills will help you to understand yourself better.

4. Stability: The Lesson of Support

The lesson of support attracts situations and experiences that leave a person feeling he or she is unsupported by others or feeling, as if his or her world could be ripped apart at any time.

If you are learning the lessons of stability, you may attract situations that rock your foundations of support. You may be left with an uneasy feeling that your life could fall apart or crumble at any moment. You may feel as if your life is void of support and you don't receive enough support from others especially family. The duality of this lesson is that you don't allow others to support you. You are very independent and do not ask for help; when people offer, you refuse because you don't wish to be a burden. You may feel that you are constantly making decisions to keep everything together and everybody happy, and you feel you always need to be the strong one.

Tick off the statements that reflect your childhood experiences.

	You had parents who separated, left, or died, and this rocked your family stability as a child.
	You were an only child who didn't have interaction with siblings
	Your family moved around a lot, and you didn't feel settled.
	You lost a sibling in your childhood.
	You were made to look after other siblings or were bought up by other siblings.
	You were made to be responsible from an early age and made to help others.
	You had parents who used you as their own emotional crutch and support, and they discussed all their problems with you.
	You had no responsibility as a child because your family gave you everything you desired.
	You did not have a balanced extended family network, including support from grandparents.

	You asked for help with something significant, and you were ignored or nothing was done to help you.
	You parents weren't able to show you emotional support.
	You parents did not take an interest in your social activities and never went to watch your sports games or your school activities.
	You were overly supported and smothered by family, and so you never had to support yourself.
	You left home or had to leave home at a young age.

This lesson may have attracted you to certain relationship and life experiences. Tick the statements that reflect yours.

	You have experienced a partner who was emotionally loving and supportive one minute, and completely detached and unsupportive another.
	You feel you are the strongest link in the family and wish others would step up and help more.
	You don't accept help and prefer to do everything yourself because you feel that you will burden others or that others will let you down.
	You have experienced a relationship in which your partner took everything and left you with nothing at the end of it.
	You have experience extended family issues of being under or overly supported and smothered.
	You attracted a partner who placed more value on doing things outside the family than on the family unit.
	Having a family has been an issue.
	You feel your values and opinions are not supported by others.
	You have experienced a broken home.

	You have lost a relationship due to difficulty in blending the family with two sets of children.
	You have experienced the push-pull scenario in a relationship—either you or a partner pushed the other away emotionally and then worked hard to pull the person back in.
	You support others but don't feel others support you, or you believe they will let you down.
	You neglect yourself because you are too busy supporting everyone else's wants and needs.
	You expect others to know what you need in order to feel supported.

The Feelings

If you have the lesson of stability with the lesson of support, it can leave you feeling insecure, unstable, unbalanced, unheard, doubtful, undervalued, unsupported, overbearing, smothered, or smothering.

The Lesson

If you have this lesson, you must understand that when you learn to find the balance between asking for support and accepting support, then others will be more supportive of you!

If you are learning the lesson of stability and support, it is important to:

- Work on building solid foundations and not allowing your emotions to encourage you to change direction whenever you feel emotionally unstable.
- Release the need to always be the strong one, and learn to ask for help. Often it is because you won't allow others to help you that you feel unsupported.
- Build emotional stability within yourself, and don't be a martyr. We can subconsciously use supporting others as a way to gain approval or sympathy.

- Take any new relationship slowly as you build a solid and secure foundation, especially with blended families.
- Build a solid and stable relationship by defining the family values of both parties and agreeing together how the family network will work for both of you.
- Feel confident within a relationship prior to starting a family, and have the belief in yourself that you will be able to provide a stable family environment.
- Learn not to lose yourself within the family environment so that you are not always putting everyone else's needs before your own.

5. Control: The Lesson of Freedom

The lesson of control attracts situations and experiences that leave a person questioning his or her freedom or not allowing others their own freedom and choice.

If you are learning the lesson of control, then you may attract people who are manipulative or controlling. The duality of this lesson is that you are manipulative and controlling. Ultimately, relationships may be a constant fight for control and disempowerment. This lesson can attract people that are very volatile, and life is full of opinions and arguments because disempowerment is used to try and gain control. People learning this lesson may also find it difficult to deal with change, or they may struggle with feeling emotionally unsettled, which directs their need to constantly change.

Tick off the statements that reflect your childhood experiences.

	Your parents were very strict in culture, religion, or parenting.
	Your older siblings made you do things you didn't want to do, or you made your siblings do what you wanted.
	Your parents argued constantly, or you witnessed verbal or physical abuse.
	You experienced sexual, physical, or verbal abuse.

	You are an only child who never had to share or compete with other children.
	You had no discipline, or you were disciplined quite harshly.
	You were forced to change schools or move to different locations when it wasn't what you wanted.
	You were bullied, or you were a bully.
	You were not allowed to express yourself or your creative ability.
	You were diagnosed with dyslexia, attention deficit-hyperactivity disorder (ADHD), Asperger's disorder, or autism.
	You had a parent who was quite smothering or controlling.
	You were made to do things that you didn't want to do (e.g., play a sport that you didn't enjoy).
	You were always getting into trouble for your behaviour.
	You were given a lot of freedom as a child and didn't have many rules.
	Your were forced to study or do something you didn't want to do.
	You were a rule breaker and didn't do what you were told.

This lesson may have attracted you to certain relationship and life experiences. Tick the statements that reflect yours.

	Others don't meet your high standards, and they never seem to do things correctly or as well as you do.
	You attract partners who don't allow you to have any control of finances or family decisions, or they make it difficult for you to keep in contact with family and friends.
	You have trouble making decisions, and so you allow others to make them for you.
	You attract very demanding people or partners who need to be in control to feel secure, or you use control to feel secure.

	You find that you attract others who don't agree with you or who have strong opinions, which causes disagreements.
	You have attracted verbal, mental, or physical abuse.
	You have experienced a relationship that was very difficult to get out of.
	You have had a substance abuse.
	You have suffered anorexia or bulimia.
	You don't like change, or you attract others who don't.
	You have attracted players—people in a relationship for only short-term gain.
	You are a control freak and like to be in charge or have things done your way.
	You are messy and don't give much attention to your living standards and personal standards, or you're obsessive and give too much attention to them.
	You feel very unsettled in life and are always searching for the next thing.

The Feelings

If you have the lesson of the control with the lesson of freedom, it can leave you feeling controlled, obligated, disempowered, manipulated, not allowed, rejected, restrained, forced, controlled, controlling, scattered, or sporadic.

The Lesson

If you have this lesson, you must understand that when you learn to live and let live, and you go with the natural progression and flow of life, you will find emotional freedom!

If you are learning the lesson of control and freedom, it is important to:

+ Work on areas of your life in which you have been giving away your power, or in which you are disempowering others.
+ Become comfortable with change and your emotions, and become aware of any emotions that are causing you to change direction when things get a little tough.
+ Understand that opinions are just opinions, and you don't always need to be right or judge yourself based on the opinions of others.
+ Realize that we don't need to control anything if we are secure and in alignment with who we are, and we should allow others their right to do the same.
+ Release the feeling that we need others to conform to our way, or that one way is the only way. Accept and become comfortable with our own differences and the differences of others. This is how we release control.
+ Learn to stay focused on the now and learn to go with the flow, so that the need to control or force is not required, and you allow the correct outcome to take its natural course.
+ Work through issues of abuse of any kind with a counsellor or healer to recover your sense of emotional freedom.

6. Commitment: The Lesson of Sharing

The lesson of commitment and sharing attracts situations and experiences that leave a person feeling vulnerable to sharing oneself and committing to life and others.

If you are learning the issues of commitment, then you may be commitment shy. The duality of this lesson subconsciously attracts people who will not commit to you or what you do. You may also be sabotaging your life with unrealistic expectations to avoid commitment. You may be too afraid to commit for fear of making a mistake. Or you may feel that it's easier to be uncommitted, just in case things don't turn out well and you end up getting hurt. The duality is that you may overcommit yourself, to the detriment of yourself or others.

Tick off the statements that reflect your childhood experiences.

	You have experienced a family breakup and witnessed a parent changing relationships often.
	You were an only child and didn't learn what it was like to share.
	You experienced a committed family upbringing where your parents were unhappy but stayed together for the sake of the children.
	You were let down a lot in your life by a parent who couldn't keep his or her promises and commitments.
	You were adopted.
	Your parents did not marry or make a formal commitment.
	One of your parents discovered he or she was homosexual and left the marriage for a gay relationship.
	Your parents had a happy relationship but relied heavily on you.
	Your parents were very social or community orientated, and you spent a lot of time with sitters or being dragged along to these events.
	You had two working parents who were never around, or two non-working parents who didn't commit to working opportunities.
	Someone in your extended family let you down, and your parents didn't know, didn't believe you, or ignored you.
	You spent a lot of time in the care of other extended family members (e.g., grandparents).
	You were spoilt as a child, always got what you wanted, and did what you wanted with no commitment.
	You were not made to face the consequences of your choices.
	You had to share everything as a child and never had your own things.

This lesson may have attracted you to certain relationship and life experiences. Tick the statements that reflect yours.

	You attract people who won't commit to you or end up leaving you high and dry.
	You attract relationships that you know are not right, but you enter them anyway because you subconsciously know you couldn't possibly commit to that person.
	You focus on everything that is wrong with others and what they do, and you give yourself reasons to why they are not right for you.
	You attract very selfish people, or people tell you that you are selfish.
	You attract a partner who doesn't want to move in together.
	You find people are emotionally distant towards you.
	You find that people break their commitments.
	You attract partners who want to rush into commitment and then seemingly fall out of love with you within a short period of time.
	You attract people who are scattered and don't focus, or you are scattered and can't focus.
	You make a big deal out of the need for everything to be fair and just.
	You break your own commitments to help others.
	You give and commit to others in detriment to yourself.
	You overcommit yourself, which affects your family life and relationships.

The Feelings

If you have the lesson of commitment with the lesson of sharing, it can leave you feeling selfish, selfless, unloved, pitiful, uninspired, disinterested, distant, undeserving, uninvolved, obligated. misunderstood, detached, greedy, or stingy.

The Lesson

If you have this lesson, you must understand that when you learn to be comfortable enough to share yourself with others without opinion or judgement, then others will commit and share themselves with you!

If you are learning the lesson commitment and sharing, it is important to:

- Learn not to lose yourself within the family and extended family environment so that you are not always putting everyone else's needs before your own.
- Work on the areas of your life that involve emotional commitment. Emotional commitment issues can make you think that the grass is always greener on the other side.
- Take stock of your emotional health to determine whether you are subconsciously picking the wrong kinds of relationships. Commitment-shy people often subconsciously attract those whom they couldn't possibly commit to or who are unlikely to commit to them.
- Deal with any belief systems that encourage you to believe that you will never be good enough, or that the person you are with isn't good enough. The lesson of the #6 profile can have you judging others harshly because it's easier to focus on others and have an opinion about their lives rather than look at your own.
- Define your values and know what you want, then make a commitment to work on yourself and commit to these values.
- Spend some time reviewing your values and what you want in your life. If you are in a relationship and feel yourself looking or feeling there has to be more than you have, you can then easily see whether your current partner is in alignment. It can often simply be the lesson getting in the way if you both want the same things, have the same values, and are heading in the same direction.
- Understand yourself, commit to your own values, and finish your projects.

7. Trust: The Lesson of Belief

The lesson of belief attracts situations that leave a person struggling with the ability to trust and believe in himself, his choices, and other people.

If you are learning the issues of trust, then you may find it very difficult to trust and believe that someone is being truthful or is right for you. You may struggle with trusting yourself to make the right decision, or when you have felt that you did make the right decision, you were let down. You may find that you attract trust issues in others with lying and cheating, or you have issues with lying and cheating yourself. You may find it difficult to believe in yourself and your own abilities, or you judge others on theirs. Your trust issues may have you searching for clues that others are trustworthy, and this hunt for truth may become an obsession. Because of a struggle with self-belief, you may feel that nobody believes in you. You may find that life is full of drama because you or those around you use drama to find evidence that the other person is true. This lesson can also have you trying to be saintly with believing that breaking rules will lose the acceptance and trust of others, or the duality that has you abusing the trust of others by being an obsessive rule breaker.

Your soul lesson is set up in childhood. Tick off the statements that reflect your childhood experiences.

	Your trust was taken advantage of in childhood.
	You were a very sensitive child and felt very different or left out.
	You had a parent who consistently warned you that the opposite sex could never be trusted, or who taught you sex was dirty or bad.
	You experienced sexual, physical, or verbal abuse.
	You had spiritual experiences as a child, but no one believed you, or people made you feel it was a negative experience.
	Your parents often made promises that they were unable to keep.
	You were bought up with very strong religious or cultural views.

	Your parents never trusted you, or they placed too much trust in you.
	You spent a lot of time alone as a child.
	You were scared of the dark (or had some similar fear) and were made to be brave or put up with it without emotional support.
	You were often not believed when you were telling the truth.
	You struggled with belief that you could do what other kids could do.
	You are always searching for proof in order to accept.
	Your upbringing was full of emotional drama.
	You were a rule breaker
	You were reprimanded or punished a lot as a child, even when you felt you did nothing to deserve it.
	Your upbringing was one where you always had to follow the rules, and disrespect for others was not tolerated.

This lesson may have attracted you to certain relationship and life experiences. Tick the statements that reflect yours.

	You attract partners who are secretive or lead double lives.
	You have experienced times of anxiety as you question what others' motives are.
	You are obsessive about checking every detail in your life or in the lives of others.
	You have trust issues.
	You have experienced emotional, physical, or mental abuse.
	You or a partner had an affair.
	You have experienced painful emotional rejections.
	You find it very difficult to express your emotions and feelings.

	You attract people with values and spiritual and cultural beliefs that are different than your own.
	You don't believe in what others tell you, even when they give you a compliment.
	You don't share your feelings and emotions for fear people will reject you or won't believe you.
	You live in your comfort zone as you struggle with your own self-belief.
	You stick to all the rules and get agitated with others when they break them.
	You tell little white lies.
	You are trying to be perfect or saintly for fear of karma, or Gods punishment.

The Feelings

If you have the soul lesson of trust with the lesson of belief, it may leave you feeling untrusted, lied to, taken advantage of, let down, forsaken, rejected, deserted, unbelieved, blamed, victimized, saintly, liable, persecuted, superior, virtuous, righteous, arrogant, or patronising.

The Lesson

If you have this lesson, you must understand that when you trust and believe in yourself, others will trust and believe in you too!

If you are learning the lesson of trust and belief, it is important to:

+ Find your inner trust of self and confidence. You can't trust anyone else when you do not trust in yourself.
+ Get in touch with your feelings and emotions, and practise self-expression. As a #7 profile, you can find it difficult to express emotions, which you mask because you are quite sensitive.

+ Learn to openly express your emotions without fear of rejection or consequences.

+ Discover what your spiritual beliefs are, and your strong intuition will guide you towards trusting in a higher order and your creator. This is very spiritual number that directs you to your true essence and spiritual nature.

+ Learn to trust that all is in perfect order, and that you can only be where you are right now and you are fine. The #7 profile energy can be very impatient, so learning to accept the now will stop you from trying to make things happen—an exercise that usually ends in disaster.

+ Focus on the positive aspects of your partner and allow him or her the right to be considered trustworthy until he or she has shown otherwise.

+ Understand that it's okay to make mistakes and that you're not in this physical existence to be perfect or saintly. Trying to be so can result in you harbouring feelings of unforgiveness, shame, and guilt.

+ Work through issues of abuse of any kind with a counsellor or healer to recover your ability to trust.

8. Security: The Lesson of Achievement

The lesson of achievement attracts situations and experiences that affect a person's ability to achieve his or her dreams and goals.

If you are learning issues of security, you may find that you attract circumstances in which money is always a focus and often an issue. You may find that others rely on you financially or are focused more on making money than an emotional connection with you. The duality of this is that you may have issues with supporting yourself financially or having the confidence to follow your own dreams. You may feel that your achievements are never good enough due to an obsessive-compulsive desire for perfection. The duality is that you lack the drive required to achieve your dreams. You may attract others who don't believe in or support your dreams, work, or business. Work-life balance is also important for this lesson, because success can often be used as compensation for a lack of emotional connection.

Your soul lesson is set up in childhood. Tick off the statements that reflect your childhood experiences.

	You grew up in a family situation in which there was no money, or you were born into a very rich family where you had no money responsibility.
	You siblings were supported and given more than you as a child.
	You left home very young and had to become financially independent.
	You had ideas and dreams as a child, and your parents didn't support them or ridiculed them.
	Money or business fascinated you as a child.
	Your family went bankrupt or lost a lot of money.
	You feel your parents were focused more on their work commitments than on you.
	You had to do a lot for your family around the home or in a business, and you didn't get to enjoy your childhood.
	You felt jealous of other kids and what they had compared to you.
	You were told you were not smart enough to achieve or do something you wanted to do.
	You were very bright at school, but you didn't have many friends or were picked on because you were smart.
	You were diagnosed with obsessive compulsive disorder or had very high expectations of yourself as child.
	You suffered an eating disorder.

This lesson may have attracted you to certain relationship and life experiences. Tick the statements that reflect yours.

	Your finances are always an issue.
	On divorce or separation, your partner was not fair, and you lost money in the settlement or in court costs.

	You attract situations in which you have to work rather than be able to stay at home and rear your family.
	You have had to take on the financial responsibility of rearing the children.
	You have no control over your finances.
	You had dreams of owning your own business, studying, or working, but others told you that you couldn't do it, or you didn't have the confidence to follow through.
	You have squandered a lot of money because you have used it to try to feel secure and worthy in the eyes of others.
	You feel like you are the only one who is always working hard.
	You have gone into a relationship because of money and security instead of your true feelings.
	You have been targeted by a con artist partner looking for financial gain.
	You are a perfectionist and get disappointed when others don't live up to your high standards.
	You are successful in achievement, but your relationships have suffered.
	You have everything you wish for, but you are not happy.
	You have an eating disorder.
	You look for reassurance in your own achievement by comparing yourself to others.
	You have a lack of desire of desire to achieve anything, and you use excuses to stay in your comfort zone.
	You have had a business fail, or you lost a lot of money.

The Feelings

If you have the soul lesson of security with the lesson of achievement, it may leave you feeling vulnerable, insecure, unreliable, unsupported, exposed, unprotected, undefended, devalued, defeated, obsessive, underrated, unrecognised, unreliable, unstable, failure, arrogant, superficial, condescending, or proud.

The Lesson

If you have this lesson, you must understand that when you allow yourself to achieve your goals and dreams with emotional balance, and when you don't use your achievements as a way to feel better about yourself or superior to others, then you will achieve success in life and relationships!

If you are learning the lesson of security and achievement, it is important to:

+ Have an understanding of the energy of money, and take any negative emotional meaning out of it. You cannot use money to build your sense of self or to make yourself happy. You will achieve great abundance, but not until you learn that you cannot sacrifice your self-love or others in the process.
+ Build your inner strength and confidence as you master the power of the skills you have been given and learnt.
+ Learn to find balance in your expectations. As a #8 profile, you can have perfectionist tendencies and often raise the bar higher than necessary. This is why you become successful. But you must realize that true love and happiness are not perfect, and that others don't always have your same high expectations.
+ Learn to not use your high expectations as an excuse for why others are never good enough. This really means you don't believe you are good enough.
+ Have the courage to follow your dream of creating your own security by connecting to your gifts, if that is what you wish. Don't allow others to tell you that your dreams are not achievable. If anyone is going to create success, it will be the #8 profile.
+ Connect to your inner strength and the power to strive forward in your chosen field, in order to create your own abundance and security. Then form a relationship in which this is supported and accepted but not expected.

+ Strive to achieve a good work-life balance; you might have a tendency to create abundance as a substitute for emotional giving.

9. Humility: The Lesson of Giving and Receiving

The lesson of giving and receiving attracts situations that leave a person feeling as if he or she is constantly being short-changed by life and others.

If you are learning the lesson of giving and receiving, you may find that you attract varying degrees of giving and receiving issues. You may find that you attract people who are very self-centred and materialistic, or you are very self-centred and materialistic. You may be a kind and caring person who gives too much and receives nothing in return. You may attract people or partners who take advantage of this giving nature and expect you to constantly give, or vice versa. You may also find that life becomes a struggle if your projection of status and how you look in society causes feelings that you haven't got or will never get what you want.

Your soul lesson is set up in childhood. Tick off the statements that reflect your childhood experiences.

	You grew up in a family in which you had little or were given little, and you felt other kids had more than you.
	You were picked on and teased for the way you looked or the clothes you wore.
	You had to work hard to help out the family.
	You were constantly told it is better to give than to receive.
	Your parents were not very giving, or they gave you everything you wanted.
	Your parents had community-based jobs that took them away from the family because of shift work.
	Your parents always had time for others but not for you.

	You loved animals as a child but were not allowed to have a pet, or you had one that was taken from you or died soon after getting it.
	The gifts you received as a child were always a letdown—either you didn't get what you wanted, it broke, or it was taken away.
	You were selfish and didn't like sharing as a child.

This lesson may have attracted you to certain relationship and life experiences. Tick the statements that reflect yours.

	You have attracted people or partners who were not very giving and yet expected a lot from you, or vice versa.
	You feel very alone in life because you feel no one is there to give to you.
	You have feel your needs are inferior to the needs of others, and you find it difficult to ask for what you want.
	You keep people at arm's length because you feel the other person always has an ulterior motive or wants something from you.
	You have very humanitarian values that support people, the earth, or animals, and you get very frustrated when people don't hold the same view.
	You feel you are never given recognition, acknowledgement, or support for what you do.
	You want to "fix" or change people, or you want people to "fix" or change you.
	You are embarrassed by others because of the way they look, what they do, or how they act or dress, or you have had others be embarrassed about you.
	You don't know how to receive.
	You apologise a lot.
	You invest too much in the outcomes and emotional lives of others.

	You give help to others in detriment to self.
	You have high expectations of family and friends and expect they should be there for you.
	You can't say no.

The Feelings

If you have the soul lesson of humility and the lesson of giving and receiving, it may leave you feeling unprovided for, ignored, used, overlooked, unnoticed, disregarded, snubbed, overworked, exploited, demanding, presuming, or conceited.

The Lesson

If you have this lesson, you must understand that when you learn to give and receive in balance and with gratitude and humility, and you don't use giving as a way to gain status or to feel better about your life, then you will receive more than you ever dreamed possible!

If you are learning the lesson of humility and giving and receiving, it is important to:

+ Come to an understanding that you are perfect just the way you are, and it's not the way you look or what you have that makes you whole.
+ Discover the true meaning of giving, and learn to give unconditionally, expecting nothing in return. When this energy is balanced, it is automatic that you will receive from the universe. It's the energy of giving with the expectation of what you can get—or should get—in return that blocks this energy.
+ Realise that if you are giving only to obtain recognition or emotional support, then you are not giving unconditionally. Look deeper into why you are giving. If you are frustrated because no one recognizes or gives to you, then your giving and receiving are out of balance.

- Ensure you receive gracefully when someone offers you something or wants to do something for you. Don't reject these gifts. If receiving is uncomfortable for you, then your giving and receiving are out of balance. Learn to say thanks gracefully without the "Oh, you shouldn't have." That statement rejects the gift and implies that you are not worth it.
- Connect to your gratitude for all the little things in your life. When you are grateful for what you have, you receive more.
- Learn to allow others to take responsibility for their own lives and their choices when constantly giving to them or rescuing them is a determent to you. You don't help people by rescuing them; you help them by teaching them how to rescue themselves. Otherwise, they will just need rescuing again.
- Do not be held to emotional ransom, or hold others to emotional ransom. As a #9 profile, you are a caring person and want everyone to be okay. You must learn that people are responsible for themselves, and the consequences of each person's choices are that individual's responsibility. Threatening consequences to get a desired outcome can be emotional blackmail.
- Learn to say no when you are made to feel obligated to do something you don't want to do. If you say yes, you will not be giving unconditionally or lovingly, and this affects you in a negative way.

Let's do a review.

An emotional reaction will cause feelings within you that align to your soul lessons. There are a lot of people who are not comfortable with their feelings and find them difficult to express. If that's you, then you are not alone. Learning to easily identify with our feelings will take practise, but the more comfortable you are with them, the more comfortable you will be with expressing them, and the less they are going to trigger your emotional reactions.

As you have worked your way through this chapter, you will have discovered your own personal blueprint and profile and your soul lessons. You have ticked off the lists and learnt how they have been set up and experienced in childhood, as well as how they have been showing up since. This is a little exercise to help you make conscious contact with your past programming and understand where it has come from.

In the next chapter, I have made it really easy for you. I have given you a list of all the relationship blueprints and profiles for every soul lesson combination and the feelings and behaviours these emotional filters combinations can create. You simply need to look up your own soul lesson combination. I have also created an "I am" affirmation and statement for each soul lesson combination that you can use to reprogram your beliefs system. There is more about this later in the book.

CHAPTER 5

Soul Lesson Combinations for All Soul Lesson Profiles

A person often meets his destiny on the road he took to
avoid it.

—Jean de La Fontaine

In this chapter, you will be able to view your soul lesson combinations and what your unique soul lesson combination is learning. I have included each combination's emotional filters and the most likely feelings and behaviours they cause.

Important Information about Your Emotional Filters

Your emotional filters are inbuilt programs and beliefs through which you perceive situations. This can cause certain feelings and patterns of behaviour that become habitual in your life. The ego is defensive and wants to protect you from your pain, and so it is sensitive to certain feelings that have been set up from your soul lessons and past experiences. Your past and your ego's sensitivity to it create your emotional filter feelings through which you then perceive all experiences. This is how three people can have the exact same experience but perceive it very differently. It is the sensitivity of this emotional filter that will determine how much of a reaction you will have to your soul lessons, and how often you are going to repeat the same emotional pattern and experience. It is this emotional filter that can create the exact experience from which the ego is trying to protect itself.

You experience these emotional patterns through all the relationships in your life. Remember that I am referring to all relationships, not just partners and family members.

There is not just one emotional filter for each combination; there are many ways to experience an inner programmed belief and emotional habit. This is where I would like you to sit with your combination, dig deep, and be truly honest with yourself. If you don't face the parts you don't like about yourself, then you can't change them. It's hard to admit to ourselves that we can be emotionally manipulative at times, or that we are not always coming from our best intentions. A lot of this is not conscious; you may not even be aware that you are doing it. The job of the ego is to protect you from perceived threats and feelings of pain, blame, shame, guilt, or fear. Because of the discomfort these feelings create, a lot of people's egos will feel defensive or may even go into denial mode. We can't grow and change from there.

We can only learn and grow when we own our stuff and start to acknowledge that which is within, as uncomfortable as this can be. It is important to recognise that everyone has issues. I have never met someone who hasn't, because we are all living in this world with an ego. Our egos can convince us that we are the only ones who ever did it tough or felt it this bad, but I can guarantee you someone will have done it tougher.

With each feeling and behaviour listed for your combination, sit with each statement and determine whether you can see yourself within it; highlight the ones where you do. Because there is duality, you may be learning one side that is more apparent. However, you can't have one side without the other, as the law suggests, so there may be hidden aspects within you too. This doesn't mean all the filters will be relevant; simply find the duality of the ones that you feel are right for you. In the next chapter, we will use these emotional filters and their behaviours to help you identify what you may have been missing and what is keeping you stuck, so that you can finally move forward.

You will also notice that some feelings and behaviours can be normal at times in our lives. For example, we can all feel like a failure at times when we don't win. However, if you had the lesson of achievement, feeling like a failure can be devastating and create emotional unbalance. In these kinds of statements, it is the emotional reaction that comes with the feeling. If it causes an emotional reaction rather than just a disappointment, it is a reaction to your emotional filter, and it is what you are learning in order to grow and evolve.

I have started at the 4 lesson because soul lessons for the 1990s and onwards don't go lower than this, and I finished at 48 because lessons don't go higher than this.

Look up your own soul lesson combination and discover you unique learning. Highlight the emotional filters, feelings, and behaviours relevant to your profile's combination.

4

Lesson: Stability/Support

Teaching: If you have this lesson you must understand that when you learn to find the balance between asking for support and accepting support, then others will be more supportive of you!

The emotional filters, feelings, and behaviours: You feel unsupported by others. You don't support others. You find it difficult to ask for and accept support. You support others in detriment to yourself. You feel that if you don't support others, their world or your world would fall apart. You feel that you don't get enough help. You don't ask for help. You expect others should know what you need. You feel like no one is ever there for you. You support others so much your own life and health suffers.

Personal Mantra: I am loved and supported in all that I do.

5

Lesson: Control/Freedom

Teaching: If you have this lesson, you must understand that when you learn to live and let live and go with the natural progression and flow of life, you will find emotional freedom!

The emotional filters, feelings, and behaviours: You feel you are always being told what to do. Being told what to do makes you angry. You are a control freak. You don't feel you have any freedom. You manipulate others to gain the upper hand. You feel manipulated by others. You feel your life is all over the place. You have high expectations of yourself. You have high expectations of others. You have an eating disorder. You are obsessive or compulsive. You are opinionated, or you feel others try to force their beliefs, values, or opinions on you.

Personal Mantra: I am surrendering and going with the flow of life.

6

Lesson: Commitment/Sharing

Teaching: If you have this lesson, you must understand that when you learn to be comfortable enough to share yourself with others without opinion or judgement, then others will commit and share themselves with you!

The emotional filters, feelings, and behaviours: You fear commitment. You find it difficult to commit to and finish things. You overcommit yourself. You attract people who won't keep their commitments. You don't keep your commitments. You share too much with others. You don't know how to share. You find it difficult to share your emotions and feelings with others. You are lazy or undercommitted.

Personal Mantra: I am committed to my dreams and to myself in balance.

7

Lesson: Trust/Belief

Teaching: If you have this lesson, you must understand that when you trust and believe in yourself, others will also trust and believe in you!

The emotional filters, feelings, and behaviours: You don't believe in yourself. You have a problem trusting others. You tell little white lies. You don't feel you can trust others enough to share your feelings. You don't believe you can do what you would love to do. You don't trust your decisions. You search for evidence that others are being truthful. You feel others always have an ulterior motive. You feel you will punished if you do something that is not truthful or breaking the law. You are too serious or try to be saintly.

Personal Mantra: I am trusting and believing in myself.

8

Lesson: Security/Achievement

Teaching: If you have this lesson, you must understand that when you allow yourself to achieve your goals and dreams with emotional balance, and you don't use your achievements to feel better about yourself or superior to others, then you will achieve success in life and relationships.

The emotional filters, feelings, and behaviours: You place a lot of pressure on yourself to succeed and be the best. You have high expectations of yourself. You have high expectations of others. You don't feel secure unless you are achieving. If you don't have money you don't feel secure. You push yourself to work harder than others. You push yourself to be a winner. If you don't succeed or win, you feel like a failure. Your work, business, or career has taken over your life. You are lazy. You are uninspired. Your stability comes from others. You rely on others financially, and the thought of doing your own thing creates fear.

Personal Mantra: I am manifesting and achieving all my desires effortlessly and easily.

9

Lesson: Humility/Giving and Receiving

Teaching: If you have this lesson, you must understand that when you learn to give and receive in balance with gratitude and humility, and you don't use giving for gain or to feel better about your life, then you will receive more than you ever dreamed possible!

The emotional filters, feelings, and behaviours: You give in detriment to self. You find it difficult to accept and ask for help. You feel like you are always the giver, and no one gives to you. You get upset when others don't give in return or are fair. You place a lot of emphasis on being fair and just. You give to others to make yourself feel better. You give and help others even when they don't ask for it. You help others too much, and so they don't need to be responsible and stand on their own two feet. You hold the view that it's better to always give than to receive.

Personal Mantra: I am grateful for all that I have and all that I receive.

10 = 1

Lessons: Independence/Abandonment, Codependence/Attention, and Repeated/Not Completed

Teaching: This soul lesson combination will have you learning and discovering the importance of self and your inner power. It is important that you understand your own value and follow your own direction without the need to rely on external sources to validate you or give you confidence.

You may find it difficult to stand in your own power and stand up for your own rights and values. Alternatively, if you force your values and opinions on others, you may need to bring this into balance.

The emotional filters, feelings, and behaviours: You abandon yourself for others. Your emotionally needy or rely heavily on others. You are opinionated and do not listen to others. You feel like you are not listened to. You are emotionally distant or detached from others for fear of being let down or hurt. You need your feelings validated by others. You believe others should make you happy. You find it difficult to validate another person's value. You use addictive or codependent behaviour to feel better. You give your heart too easily, or you don't let others in.

Personal Mantra: I am owning my life, and my happiness comes from within.

11 = 2

Lessons: Independence/Abandonment and Codependence/Attention

Teaching: This soul lesson combination will have you learning and discovering the importance of self and your inner power. It is important that you understand your own value and follow your own direction without the need to rely on external sources to validate you or give you confidence.

You may find it difficult to stand in your own power and stand up for your own rights and values. Alternatively, if you force your values and opinions on others, you may need to bring this into balance. The doubled energy of independence and abandonment tells you that you will be slightly more sensitive to this lesson, and abandonment may be a very strong fear within you.

The emotional filters, feelings, and behaviours: You abandon yourself for others. You're emotionally needy or rely heavily on others. You are opinionated and do not listen to others. You feel like you are not listened to. You are emotionally distant or detached from others for fear of being let down or hurt. You need your feelings validated by others. You believe others should make you happy. You find it difficult to validate other people's value. You use addictive or codependent behaviour to feel better. You give your heart too easily, or you don't let others in. You require constant reassurance.

Personal Mantra: I am owning my life, and my happiness comes from within.

12 = 3

Lessons: Independence/Abandonment, Codependence/Attention, and Self-worth/Acceptance

Teaching: This soul lesson combination will have you learning the three lessons of self. You are learning to own your personal power and build your confidence from within, without the need to rely on external sources to validate you or your worth.

You may find it difficult to stand in your own power and stand up for your own rights and values. Alternatively, if you force your values and opinions on others, you may need to bring this into balance. You are learning not to use self-criticism and the criticism of others to mask your own lack of personal power and self-love. You are learning that you don't need to prove your worth or have others prove theirs in order to gain acceptance. You are learning not to abandon yourself in the process of making others feel worthier or to gain attention. You are learning to say no and to have a voice without being opinionated. You are learning not to feel abandoned or unworthy if you don't get the attention or validation you are expecting. You are learning everyone has different values. You are learning not to take everything to heart and that not everything is always about you. You are learning other people's behaviours are not a reflection of you but of them. You are learning you don't always need to be perfect to feel worthy. You are learning that you can't expect others to give you what you cannot give yourself. You are learning the balance between being needy and nonaffectionate. You are learning that when issues arise, you need to clarify, and you are learning you don't need to gain approval for your actions, thoughts, and beliefs.

The emotional filters, feelings, and behaviours: You don't feel good enough, or what you do is ever good enough. You find it difficult to stand up for yourself. You may be critical of others, overanalyse, and judge them and what they do. You unconsciously shut out people when they make you feel insecure or persecuted. You allow other people's opinions and judgements of you to affect your self-esteem. You feel like everyone else thinks that nothing you ever do is good enough. You abandon yourself, trying to prove yourself to others. You are emotionally needy or rely heavily on others. You do not listen to others. You feel like you're not listened to. You don't feel worthy of love. You require external sources to validate your worth. You use addictive means or codependent behaviour to feel better. You require constant reassurance that you are accepted. You feel like you don't fit in. You feel that if you are beautiful or perfect, you will fit in and be accepted. You change your values and behaviour to suit others so that you are accepted and fit in. You rebel against others and the status quo, and you don't want to fit in. You use negative attention to stand out and show you don't need the acceptance of others to fit in. You disconnect from others and keep others at a distance. You don't like people and prefer to be alone. You prefer to be alone so that you won't be judged or criticised. Your oversensitive and suffer anxiety. You are uncaring and don't have much compassion. You suffer social anxiety. You feel you're different and no one ever understands or gets you.

Personal Mantra: I am confident and worthy of acceptance and loving attention.

13 = 4

Lessons: Independence/Abandonment, Codependence/Attention, Self-worth/Acceptance, and Stability/Support

Teaching: This lesson combination will have you learning not to judge or measure your own self-worth against the amount of support and stability you feel you have or haven't received. You will learn that you are worthy of support and that you don't always need to be the strong one. You will learn to ask for support in a balanced way. You will learn to look at the part you play in creating the amount of support you receive in your life. You may be subconsciously keeping others away with independence, or relying heavily on others for support because of your own lack of confidence. You are learning to stand in your power with confidence, and that you don't need to prove anything to yourself or others in order to receive support or feel worthy.

The emotional filters, feelings, and behaviours: You feel like you are not supported or don't deserve support. You feel like you support everyone else, but no one cares about you. You feel abandoned by others when they don't support you. You abandon others when they need support. You don't stand up for yourself for fear of criticism or judgement. You feel others will think you're not good enough if you ask them for help. You overly support others to make yourself feel better about you or your life. You abandon yourself and your goals to be there for others. You feel like you're the support person for others, and they rely too heavily on you. You feel like your dreams are rejected by others unless it suits them. You feel like you're the main creator of stability, and if you don't support everyone, your world will come crashing down. If you don't get the validation from others you seek, you feel others don't think you're doing a good enough job, or you feel unsupported.

Personal Mantra: I am worthy of love, acceptance, and support.

14 = 5

Lessons: Independence/Abandonment, Codependence/Attention, Stability/Support, and Control/Freedom

Teaching: This soul lesson combination will have you learning that you cannot find support and attention through manipulating and controlling others, or through allowing yourself to be manipulated or controlled. You will learn that by being yourself and allowing both yourself and others the freedom to experience life as all desire, it will result in the support and validation you seek. You will also learn to stand in your power and not allow the opinions and judgement of others to control the way you support and treat yourself. You may need to learn that others won't always abandon you if you don't offer the support they want. You are learning not to use the support you give to others as a way to feel more loved. You are learning not to use the amount of support you receive from others as a measure of their love. You are learning not to abandon yourself for everyone else. You are learning that manipulation can't be used to get the outcome you want. You are learning you have no control over the behaviour of others, and you are not responsible for fixing others.

The emotional filters, feelings, and behaviours: You feel like you have no control over the support you get from others. You feel like others emotionally control you to give them support. You feel like you're abandoned by others when they don't support you. You abandon others when they need support. You fear standing up for yourself and asking for support. You feel others will think you are not in control of your own life if you ask for help. You overly support others to validate yourself or because you fear abandonment. You abandon yourself and your goals to support others. You feel like your need for support is rejected by others unless it suits them. You give support to manipulate or control others in order to get what you want. You fear if you don't give others support, they won't love you or will abandon you.

Personal Mantra: I am lovingly supported and free to be me.

15 = 6

Lessons: Independence/abandonment, Codependence/Attention, Control/Freedom, and Commitment/Sharing

Teaching: This soul lesson combination will have you learning that control and abandonment cannot be used to gain commitment from others. You are learning not to overcommit yourself and abandon your own life for everyone else. You are learning not to control others to get what you want. You may be learning that you use overcommitting to others to gain attention or validation from them. You may need to learn that you manipulate others to commit to you and do what you want by giving them attention and external validation. You are learning not to seek constant reassurance from others of their committed to you to feel stable. You are learning that the amount of commitment people show you is not what you base their love and approval of you on. You are learning that if you don't get the attention you think you need from others, it's not always a measure of their commitment or a sign they will abandon you.

The emotional filters, feelings, and behaviours: You feel you have no control over the amount of commitment someone is giving you. You abandon your own commitments because you fear standing up to a manipulative person. You overcommit to gain attention or control. You undercommit to feel free. You constantly make changes and don't finish what you start. You stay in a relationship or job situation for fear of change or being on your own. You feel commitment means control, and when you commit, you feel you lose your independence or freedom. You commit quickly and lose your sense of self to those who give you positive attention or love. You feel that the amount of commitment someone shows you is based on how much they love or care about you. You feel that if people don't give you the attention you need, they aren't committed to you or are going to abandon you. You feel family and others demand your attention and commitment, and you have no control over your life.

Personal Mantra: I am free to lovingly commit to myself and my dreams.

16 = 7

Lessons: Independence/Abandonment, Codependence/Attention, Commitment/Sharing, and Trust/Belief

Teaching: This soul lesson combination will have you learning to trust and commit to the belief in yourself, and when you do, others will also commit and believe in you too. You will learn that you can't use the amount of attention and validation you get from others to form your beliefs and perceptions about their commitment or belief in you. This soul lesson combination can also teach you to believe in and commit to yourself so that others will too. It is teaching you that when you abandon yourself to commit more to other people's beliefs and ideas, you will be taken off your path. This lesson is teaching you to trust yourself and commit to yourself more. You are learning not to overcommit to others in detriment to yourself, your life, and your health. You are learning to step up in your commitments if you are being lazy and uninspired. You are learning to trust and believe that someone will commit to you.

The emotional filters, feelings, and behaviours: You struggle to trust that others will hold their commitments to you or commit to you. You don't believe that there is anyone for you. You don't commit to others for a fear of getting hurt. You abandon your instinct and commit to others because you have more belief in them than your own instinct. You abandon your commitments because after a while, you don't believe in them or you. You follow other people's beliefs and hold them higher than your own. You get attention from affairs or cheating. You fear being abandoned or cheated on. You tell little white lies to keep everyone happy. You lie to yourself about your own commitments and happiness. You overcommit to others because you don't want to let anyone down. You execute your commitments in a martyr fashion so that you don't risk bad attention or karma. Your are too serious or too saintly.

Personal Mantra: I am committing to myself because I trust and believe in me.

17 = 8

Lessons: Independence/Abandonment, Codependence/Attention, Trust/Belief, and Security/Achievement

Teaching: This soul lesson combination will have you learning to value and believe in yourself and your ability to manifest and achieve what you would love in your life. You are learning that your achievement and success does not come from outside of you. You are learning that when you discover self-belief and self-love, you will create a magical and abundant life. You are also learning that you can't force your beliefs on others to feel more secure in your own. When you abandon your own beliefs for the beliefs of others, you will learn that you won't find the security you seek, and you will feel insecure. You are learning it's okay to make mistakes, and you don't need to be so serious or saintly. You are learning that you can achieve your dreams by connecting to your inner world. You are learning not to abandon others in the pursuit of achievement. You are learning to connect to others and be authentic with your feelings and emotions.

The emotional filters, feelings, and behaviours: You don't believe in yourself and your ability to create your own security and achievement. You rely on external sources to make you feel secure. You feel money and finances are always an issue. You abandon yourself to follow other people's dreams. You use the amount of positive attention you get from others to affect the belief you have in yourself. You abandon your beliefs when you don't feel secure. You don't trust others will recognise your achievements. You abandon others to focus on your achievements because you believe success will make you happy. You base your happiness on the amount of success or achievement you have in your life. You don't believe you deserve to be successful or achieve your dreams. You don't believe you deserve money or security. You hold the belief that you can't be spiritual and rich. You judge others or are jealous of others for their status and wealth.

Personal Mantra: I am secure in my self-belief, and I am achieving all my dreams.

18 = 9

Lessons: Independence/Abandonment, Codependence/Attention, Security/Achievement, and Humility/Giving and Receiving

Teaching: This soul lesson combination will have you learning to value your own achievement from within and to not use giving and receiving as a way to validate yourself. You will gain more security and achievement in your life when giving and receiving is not used to find your inner happiness or to gain attention. You may also be learning that you can't rely on others to give you the security that you cannot give yourself, or that you shouldn't abandon yourself in the process of giving security to others. This lesson is teaching you to keep your giving and receiving in balance, or else you will not feel secure. You are learning that when you overly give to others, they do not have to learn to be responsible for themselves. You are learning not to give in detriment to your own health and life. You are learning to give unconditionally in balance. You are learning abundance comes when you take out what's in it for you and focus more on the service. You are learning that when you rely on others to provide your security, you will not feel validated or secure.

The emotional filters, feelings, and behaviours: You use giving and receiving to make yourself feel good or feel secure. You abandon yourself and your own dreams to be there for others. You abandon others to follow your own achievements and dreams. You rely on others to support you financially. You don't know how to receive; it makes you feel uncomfortable. You base your happiness on your financial security. You financially support others in detriment to self. You feel secure only when people are giving to you or when you're achieving. You have high expectations of what others should be able to do and achieve, or you have these high expectations on yourself. You place too much attention on money rather than service and giving. You place too much attention on giving to others, and it affects you financially. You believe that it's better to give than to receive, and you feel guilty about receiving. People giving to you makes you feel uncomfortable. You feel that others always have an ulterior motive if they give to you. You feel rejected if someone doesn't give you the attention you need or support your achievements and goals.

Personal Mantra: I am giving and receiving in balance and achieving all that I wish to achieve.

19 = 10 = 1

Lessons. Independence/Abandonment, Codependence/Attention, Humility/Giving and Receiving, and Repeated/Not Completed

Teaching: This soul lesson combination will have you learning and discovering humility balanced with the importance of self and your inner power. It is important that you understand your own value and follow your own direction, with humble intentions towards giving and receiving. You are learning not to give in detriment to self, and also to humbly give in service to others. You will learn that you can't always rely on external sources to validate you or give you what you need. You may find it difficult to stand in your own power and stand up for your own rights and values. Alternatively, if you force your values and opinions on others, you may need to bring this into balance. You are learning that giving and receiving must be balanced, or you will lose yourself and others will not give you the attention you need. You are learning to say no and to not give in detriment to yourself or your life. You are learning to gratefully accept from others. You are learning you don't always have to be the strong one. You are learning that you have an inner power and don't need to rely on others.

The emotional filters, feelings, and behaviours: You abandon yourself by giving too much to others. You're emotionally needy or rely heavily on others. You are opinionated and do not listen to others. You feel like you are not listened to. You are emotionally distant or detached from others and fear being taken advantage of. You need your feelings or what you are giving in life to be validated by others. You believe others should make you happy by giving to you. You find your happiness by overgiving to others. You find it difficult to receive. You use addictive or codependent behaviour to feel good. If people don't give you what you want, you abandon them or feel abandoned. You use the amount of giving and receiving you get from others as a measure of their love for you. You try to help others when it's not asked for. You get frustrated when people don't listen to the advice you give. You get upset when others don't give in return or are unfair. You place a lot of emphasis on being fair and just. You give to others to make yourself feel better about your life or to feel connected. You keep others away because you fear being let down or hurt.

Personal Mantra: I am giving and receiving in balance and owning my own life and happiness.

20

Lessons: Codependence/Attention, Independence/Abandonment, and Repeated/Not Completed

Teaching: This soul lesson combination will have you learning and discovering the importance of self and your inner power. It is important you understand your own value and follow your own direction without the need to rely on external sources for this validation or to help you feel better about yourself and your life.

You may find it difficult to stand in your own power and stand up for your own rights and values. Alternatively, if you force your values and opinions on others, you may need to bring this into balance. You are learning to not abandon yourself for everyone else. You are learning to not allow others to become codependent on you, because you are keeping them from learning to take responsibility.

The emotional filters, feelings, and behaviours: You abandon yourself for others. You're emotionally needy or rely heavily on others. You are opinionated and don't listen to others. You feel like you are not listened to. You are emotionally distant or detached from others for fear of being let down or hurt. You need your feelings validated by others. You believe others should make you happy. You find it difficult to validate other people's feelings or value. You use addictions or codependent behaviour to feel better. You give your heart too easily, rush into new relationships, and then abandon them or get abandoned just as quickly. Relationships are volatile, and one party uses attention and drama to gain proof of the other person's love. Relationships resemble the push-pull scenario, where one party pushes away just so one can pull the other back in for proof of love.

Personal Mantra: I am owning my life, and my happiness comes from within.

21 = 3

Lessons: Codependence/Attention, Independence/Abandonment, and Self-worth/Acceptance

Teaching: This soul lesson combination will have you learning the three lessons of self. You are learning to own your personal power and build your confidence from within, without the need to rely on external sources to validate you or your worth.

You may find it difficult to stand in your own power and stand up for your own rights and values. Alternatively, if you force your values and opinions on others, you may need to bring this into balance. You are learning not to use self-criticism and the criticism and judgement of others to mask your own lack of personal power and self-love. You are learning that you don't need to prove your self-worth or have others prove theirs, in order to gain acceptance. You are learning not to abandon yourself in the process of making others feel worthier or gaining attention. You are learning to say no and have a voice without being opinionated. You are learning to not feel abandoned or unworthy if you don't get the attention or validation you are expecting. You are learning everyone has different values. You are learning not to take everything personally and that not everything is always about you. You are learning other people's behaviours are not a reflection of you but of them. You are learning you don't always need to be perfect to feel worthy. You are learning that you can't expect others to give you what you cannot give yourself. You are learning the balance between being needy and non-affectionate. You are learning when issues arise, you don't need to justify and gain approval for your actions, thoughts, and beliefs.

The emotional filters, feelings, and behaviours: You don't feel good enough or believe what you do is good enough. You find it difficult to stand up for yourself. You may be critical of others and overanalyse and judge them and what they do. You unconsciously shut out people when they make you feel insecure. You allow other people's opinions and judgements of you to affect your self-esteem. You feel like everyone else thinks you're not good enough. You abandon yourself while trying to prove yourself to others. You are emotionally needy or rely heavily on others. You do not listen to others. You feel like you're not listened to. You don't feel worthy of love. You require external sources to validate your worth. You use addictive means or codependent behaviour to feel better. You require constant reassurance that you are accepted. You feel like you don't fit in. You feel that if you were beautiful or perfect, you would fit in and be accepted. You change your values and behaviour to suit others so that you are accepted and fit in. You rebel against others and the status quo, and you don't want to fit in. You use negative attention to stand out and show you don't need others acceptance or to fit in. You disconnect from others and keep others away. You don't like people and prefer to be alone. You prefer to be alone so that you won't be judged or criticised. Your oversensitive and suffer anxiety. You are uncaring and don't have much compassion. You suffer social anxiety. You feel you're different, and no one ever understands or gets you.

Personal Mantra: I am confident and worthy of acceptance and loving attention.

22 = 4

Lessons: Codependence/Attention, Independence/Abandonment, and Stability/Support

Teaching: This soul lesson combination will have you learning to find the balance between asking for support and accepting support. You are learning not to overly support others and abandon yourself to the point that your life and health suffers. You are learning that you can't support others who are not ready to support themselves. You will learn to look at the part you play in creating the amount of support you receive in your life. You may be subconsciously keeping others away with independence, or relying heavily on others for support, because you don't feel you can support yourself. You are learning to feel supported.

The emotional filters, feelings, and behaviours: You feel unsupported by others and believe that no one is ever there for you when you need. You don't support others. You find it difficult to ask for and accept support. You support others in detriment to yourself. You feel that if you didn't support others, their world or your world would fall apart. You feel that you don't get enough help. You abandon yourself and your goals to be there for others. You feel like others rely too heavily on you. You feel abandoned if you don't get the support you need from others. Your world doesn't feel stable when you need to rely on others for support. You over support others because you feel they can't support themselves, or you force your support on others when it's not asked for.

Personal Mantra: I am giving and accepting support in perfect balance.

23 = 5

Lessons: Codependence/Attention, Independence/Abandonment, Self-worth/Acceptance, and Control/Freedom

Teaching: This soul lesson combination will have you learning that you cannot find love and acceptance through manipulating and controlling others or allowing yourself to be manipulated or controlled. You will learn that by being true to yourself and allowing both yourself and others the freedom to experience free will, you'll find more acceptance both within and with others. You will also learn to stand in your power and not allow the opinions and judgement of others to affect your confidence or stop you from living the life you came here to live. You are learning not to abandon others when you feel unsettled or unvalued. You are learning to not take things so personally and to not use attention as a way to validate your worthiness. You are learning to not be a control freak and to go with the flow. You are learning to bring your high expectations of yourself and others into balance and not use them as a measure of your or others' worth. You are learning not to abandon others simply because they don't give you the attention you feel your worth. You are learning not to abandon yourself because you don't feel you are good enough or will be accepted.

The emotional filters, feelings, and behaviours: You feel like you have no control over your own happiness and life. You feel like others emotionally control you. You put up with others telling you what to do because you are scared to be on your own. You lack direction and control because of a lack of self-confidence. You don't have the confidence to follow your own direction. You feel you need to be in control. You abandon yourself and your goals because you feel others will abandon you if you don't. You manipulate or control others to get what you want. You are a control freak. You have high standards of yourself and others, feeling that nothing is ever good enough. You are obsessive or compulsive. You use attention to get what you want, and when you get it, you feel good. If you don't get positive attention from others, you feel rejected. You lack self-respect and are lazy because you don't feel worthy. You feel like you're at everyone's beck and call, or you feel if you are at others' beck and call, they will value you more. You feel you want your freedom in a relationship, but you're lonely and want a relationship when you don't have one.

Personal Mantra: I am worthy of love and respect and the freedom to be me.

24 = 6

Lessons: Codependence/Attention, Independence/Abandonment, Stability/Support, and Commitment/Sharing

Teaching: This soul lesson combination is learning that you have a voice and deserve the commitment and support of others. You are also learning the importance of committing to yourself and finding your own stability from within in the areas you have let go. You are learning that commitments should be balanced with equal support of both self and others. You are learning not to overcommit yourself and abandon your own life for everyone else. You are learning that you may be using overcommitting to others to gain attention or validation from them. You are learning not to seek constant reassurance from others in order to feel stable. You are learning that if people don't give you the support and attention you think you need, it doesn't always mean they are not committed or are going to abandon you. You are learning not to oversupport or overcommit to others because they won't learn how to be responsible for themselves.

The emotional filters, feelings, and behaviours: You feel unsupported by others through their lack of commitment. You abandon your own commitments to support others because you fear standing up for yourself. You overcommit or support others to gain attention. You undercommit due to feeling overwhelmed. You stay in a relationship or job situation for fear of letting others down. If people do not give you the support you need, you question their commitment to you. You commit quickly and lose your sense of self to those who give you positive attention or love. You have no freedom or time because you're too busy fixing everyone else. You feel you need to be there for everyone. You don't feel stable unless people validate their commitment to you. You overly support others and believe if you don't, their world will fall apart. You live your life through the support and commitment to others.

Personal Mantra: I am committed to lovingly supporting myself and others in balance.

25 = 7

Lessons: Codependence/Attention, Independence/Abandonment, Control/Freedom, and Trust/Belief

Teaching: This soul lesson combination is learning that your sensitivity doesn't mean you need to rely on confirmation from others to believe in yourself. You need to find this balance so that you don't try to change or control others or allow yourself to be changed or controlled. You are learning not to abandon yourself and your freedom for other people's values and beliefs. You are learning not to abandon others because they don't hold the same beliefs and values as you. You are learning to trust others and go with the flow, or you are learning to trust more in yourself and take more control. You are learning that you don't need to be a saint and that it's okay to make mistakes. You are learning not to be so serious and to bend the rules at times, as long as it doesn't hurt others. You are learning to believe in your inner power and to not give that power to others through becoming a victim of life. You are learning to take control of your life and believe in yourself and your inner guidance.

The emotional filters, feelings and behaviours: You find it difficult to believe in yourself, and you believe too much in the opinions and judgements of others. You are sensitive to criticism and take things personally. You feel abandoned by others when they don't give you the attention you believe they should. You fear breaking the rules or making mistakes, and you try to live too saintly. You are overly critical of others who make mistakes and are not perfect. You don't trust other people and feel they have an ulterior motive. You trust others too much and then feel let down when they don't have the same values as you. You give others positive attention to gain what you want. You believe too much in the beliefs of others and allow their beliefs to determine your own. You are easily led astray by trusting too much in others. You don't believe you can take control of your own life, and you rely heavily on others. You believe others should make you happy, and when they don't, you quickly abandon them. You allow yourself to be manipulated by others who give you positive attention. You keep others away because you believe there is no one for you, or you will be let down.

Personal Mantra: I am going with the flow and trusting and believing in myself and the process of life.

26 = 8

Lessons: Codependence/Attention, Independence/Abandonment, Commitment/Sharing, and Security/Achievement

Teaching: This soul lesson combination is learning that you can't use the commitment and attention you give to or get from others to feel secure.

You are learning that your financial contribution is not the reason someone is committed to you. You will learn that if you're seeking security through others, they may abandon you, or it may affect how you value yourself. You are learning to balance your commitments, especially work and family. You are learning that if others don't value your direction, you shouldn't abandon it too. You are learning to not devalue others because they haven't got the same work ethic or same high expectations you have. You may be learning to commit more to your own value and security. You are learning that once you value yourself and commit to what you really want to do, surrendering to the outcome, you can manifest and achieve all you desire. You are learning that a lack of commitment to your role is why you are not achieving your goals. You are learning to not overcommit to the point where your health and life suffers. You may be learning that you can't use your own financial stability to feel secure in a relationship, for fear that others won't commit to you or will abandon you if you can't pay your way.

The emotional filters, feelings, and behaviours: You abandon your own direction and commitments to be there for others, or you abandon others and their dreams with the expectation that they should commit to yours. You only feel emotional secure when you are committed to and achieving your tasks and goals. You have high expectations of yourself and others, and you demand commitment. If someone doesn't commit to your values or purpose, you shut them out. You will only commit to others if they can offer you security. You overcommit to others to make them feel more secure, and your finances suffer. You stay in jobs or change jobs often for fear of committing to your own purpose. You find commitment a challenge in your work and finances, for fear you may be abandoned by others for overachieving or underachieving. You are not achieving your goals and dreams because you are not committed to doing the work you need to do. You make a big deal out of paying your way because you feel others will abandon you if they don't, or you abandon others when they don't.

Personal Mantra: I am committed to achieving a secure future with love, balance, and harmony.

27 = 9

Lessons: Codependence/Attention, Independence/Abandonment, Trust/ Belief, and Humility/Giving and Receiving

Teaching: This soul lesson combination is learning to believe you are a good person, and this comes from within; it isn't determined by the external amount you give or receive. You are learning you can't use giving and receiving to feel good or get loving attention. You are learning to not reject or feel rejected by others when they don't have the same value of giving as you. You are learning to give unconditionally but not to the detriment to the self. You are learning to believe you deserve to receive. You may be learning you are holding back on giving because you believe others don't deserve to receive. You are learning not to rely so much on what others can do for you or give to you. You are learning to not judge others on how much you receive from them, or to not feel obligated because you believe they will abandon you. You are learning not to be a martyr or self-centred. You are learning to say no, and you are learning that people don't always have an ulterior motive to their giving. You are learning that overgiving to others will not change their behaviour or beliefs, and this also stops them from learning their own responsibilities. You are learning to believe that you are a great help to others and are valued. You are learning to not be critical and judgemental of others when they don't hold your values and beliefs.

The emotional filters, feelings, and behaviours: You give in detriment to yourself because you feel others are needier. You give to others because it's the only way you feel good and believe you are loved. You believe others will abandon you if you don't give to them. You give too much to others and disregard your own values. You don't trust in the motives of others unless you are receiving exactly what you want from them. You believe you don't give enough. You don't believe you deserve to receive, or you get jealous because you believe others have more than you. You don't trust that god, the universe, or anyone has your back. You hold the belief that it's better to give than receive. You measure a person's trust on how much attention you are receiving from them, and if it's not enough, you feel abandoned. You hold your emotions in and don't share them because you don't like emotional attention or feeling needy. You overshare your emotions because you need attention to believe you are loved. You are critical or jealous of others you feel have received more than you.

Personal Mantra: I am trusting in myself and gratefully receive love and attention in balance.

28 = 10 = 1

Lessons: Codependence/Attention, Independence/Abandonment, Security/Achievement, and Repeated/Not Completed

Teaching: This soul lesson combination will have you learning that abandoning yourself or others is not going to help you feel more secure or give you what you want. You are learning that your sense of security comes from within and not from external sources. You are also learning that you won't feel more secure by holding others away or by gaining more security and abundance. You will gain more security and achievement in your life when you find your inner happiness and learn to stand in your own power. You are learning that you can't rely on others to give you the security that you cannot give yourself, or learning not to abandon yourself and your direction for everyone else. You may also be learning that you cannot force your high standards and opinions on others to try to make them achieve more or to make you feel more secure. You may be learning that you may need to lift your own values and standards to achieve what you want. You are learning to connect more to others and to not be so independent, or you're learning to be more independent and less needy. You are learning not to abandon yourself and your health by being an over achiever.

The emotional filters, feelings, and behaviours: You abandon yourself and your dreams for others. You don't feel you can be secure or achieve your dreams in your own right. You feel others would abandon you if you did what you really wanted to do. You fear others will abandon you if you don't keep them happy. You rely on others for security because it's easier. You feel no one can do it as well as you, and so you always do it. You use achievement to gain praise and attention from others. You're an overachiever or an underachiever. You only feel good when you get positive attention or achieve at a high standard. You feel like a failure when you don't meet your own standard or don't get the praise you expected. You shut out people who don't make you feel secure or who aren't up to your standards. You're opinionated and reject others whom you consider inferior to you. You are insecure and listen to too much to the opinions of others, especially those you view as superior to you. You are an underachiever because you feel you can't meet your own or other people's expectations. You are needy and seek external sources to make you feel good. You have an addiction.

Personal Mantra: I am achieving a balanced, loving, abundant life through self-validation and connecting to others.

29 = 11 = 2

Lessons: Codependence/Attention, Humility/Giving and Receiving, and Independence/Abandonment

Teaching: This soul lesson combination has you learning to find and expand your personal power so that you don't need to use external sources of validation or giving to others to feel good about yourself or your life. You are learning to not abandon yourself by giving to everyone else. You are learning to not abandon others when they don't give you what you want. You are learning to stand in your power and give to yourself without guilt. You are learning to not be opinionated or force your opinions on others. You are learning you can't help everyone and that people must also help themselves. You are learning to receive and ask for help. You are learning to give unconditionally. You are learning to stand up for yourself and speak your truth. You are learning the more you do for others, the less they do for themselves. You are learning to say no. You are learning to follow your inner calling and to not listen to everyone else's opinion on what that is. You are learning to stand up for your rights and values. You are learning to help those who are innocent, but not in detriment to yourself. You are learning that when you are being responsible for others, they can't learn to be responsible for themselves. You are learning the balance between being needy and holding others away. You are learning that people are not always personally letting you down. You are learning the push-pull scenario in relationships, where people push others away so they can pull them back in. You are learning to not seek attention in order to feel secure. You are learning to make your own decisions and be decisive.

The emotional filters and behaviours: You find it hard to say no. You help and give to others to the detriment of yourself. You abandon your needs because you feel others are needier. You don't feel valued unless you are given praise for your deeds. If others don't agree with you or have a different opinion, you feel abandoned or let down. You abandon others if they don't agree with you or give to you. You help out even when it's not asked for. You feel if you stop helping others, they will abandon you. You get emotionally upset when those you have helped go back to their old behaviours. You live by the motto that it's much better to give than to receive. You don't know what to do for yourself, and so you keep giving to others. You don't give to yourself because you're too busy giving to others. You use giving to others to distract you from yourself or life. You help others too much, and they are not learning to be responsible for themselves. You help when your help is not requested because you feel you are needed or know better. You try to save people from their pain. You give too much, and your own life and health suffers. You put more value on what people owe you or can give you than on the relationship itself. You abandon others by not replying or shutting them out because you fear standing up for yourself.

Personal Mantra: I am standing in my personal power and lovingly giving to myself and others.

30 = 3

Lessons: Self-worth/Acceptance and Repeated/Not completed

Teaching: This soul lesson combination is learning that you are good enough and worthy of acceptance. You are learning that when you accept yourself, you will be able to accept others too. You are learning that you don't need the praise and acceptance of others to make you feel worthy. You are learning to stand up for yourself, and you're learning you have nothing to prove to yourself or others. You are learning that no one is perfect. You are learning not to accept and allow bad behaviour in your life. You are learning to allow others the right to be who they are without judgement and without it affecting you. You are learning not to judge and criticise others in order to make you feel better about yourself. You are learning the way others act towards you is not a reflection of you but of them. You are learning that everything is not always about you, and to not take things so personally. You are learning you have nothing to prove to yourself or others in order to feel worthy.

The emotional filters, feelings, and behaviours: You feel unworthy. You feel others are always judging and criticising you. You find it difficult to accept or give praise. You react when someone has a suggestion or says something with which you don't agree. You will argue to prove your worth. You find it difficult to accept the way things are. You are trying to be perfect to keep everyone happy or to be accepted. You are judgemental and find faults with everything you or others do. You tell others what to do. You take everything personally. You feel bullied. You are a bully. You twist things around so that you don't look bad. You try to be perfect so that everyone will like and accept you. You agree with everyone to keep the peace. You put up with bad behaviour. You do bad behaviour to fit in or to be accepted. You are sensitive and suffer from anxiety.

Personal Mantra: I am worthy of love and acceptance, and there is nothing I need to prove.

31 = 4

Lessons: Self-worth/Acceptance, Independence/Abandonment, Codependence/Attention, and Stability/Support

Teaching: This lesson combination will have you learning not to judge or measure your own self-worth against the amount of support and stability you feel you have or haven't received. You will learn that you are worthy of support and you don't always need to be the strong one. You will learn to ask for support in a balanced way. You will learn to look at the part you play in creating the amount of support you receive in your life. You may be subconsciously keeping others away with independence, or relying heavily on others for support, because of your own lack of confidence. You are learning to stand in your power with confidence. You don't need to prove anything to yourself or others in order to receive support or feel worthy.

The emotional filters, feelings, and behaviours: You feel like you're not supported or don't deserve support. You feel like you support everyone else, but no one cares about you. You feel abandoned by others when they don't support you. You abandon others when they need support. You don't stand up for yourself for fear of criticism or judgement. You feel others will think you're not good enough if you ask them for help. You overly support others to make yourself feel better about you or your life. You abandon yourself and your goals to be there for others. You feel like you're the support person for others, and they rely too heavily on you. You feel like your dreams are rejected by others unless it suits them. You feel like you're the main creator of stability, and if you don't support everyone, your world will come crashing down. If you don't get the validation from others you seek, you feel others don't think you're doing a good enough job, or you feel unsupported.

Personal Mantra: I am worthy of love, acceptance, and support.

32 = 5

Lessons: Self-worth/Acceptance, Codependence/Attention, Independence/Abandonment, and Control/Stability

Teaching: This soul lesson combination will have you learning that you cannot find love and acceptance through manipulating and controlling others, or by allowing yourself to be manipulated or controlled. You will learn that by being true to yourself and allowing both yourself and others the freedom to experience free will, it will result in you finding more acceptance both within and with others. You will also learn to stand in your power and not allow the opinions and judgement of others to affect your confidence and stop you from living the life you came here to live. You are learning to not abandon others when you feel unsettled or unvalued. You are learning to not take things so personally and to not use attention as a way to validate your worthiness. You are learning to not be a control freak and to go with the flow. You are learning to bring your high expectations of yourself and others into balance, and to not use them as a measure of yours or others worth. You are learning not to abandon others simply because they don't give you the attention you feel your worth. You are learning not to abandon yourself because you don't feel you are good enough or will be accepted.

The emotional filters, feelings, and behaviours: You feel like you have no control over your own happiness and life. You feel like others emotionally control you. You put up with others telling you what to do because you are scared to be on your own. You lack direction and control because of a lack of self-confidence. You don't have the confidence to follow your own direction. You feel you need to be in control. You abandon yourself and your goals because you feel others will abandon you if you don't. You manipulate or control others to get what you want. You are a control freak. You have high standards of yourself and others, and you feel that nothing is ever good enough. You are obsessive or compulsive. You use attention to get what you want, and when you get it, you feel good. If you don't get positive attention from others, you feel rejected. You lack self-respect and are lazy because you don't feel worthy. You feel like you're at everyone's beck and call, or you feel that if you are at others' beck and call, they will value you more. You feel you want your freedom in a relationship, but you're lonely and want a relationship when you don't have one.

Personal Mantra: I am worthy of love and respect and the freedom to be me.

33 = 6

Lessons: Self-worth/Acceptance and Commitment/Sharing

Teaching: This soul lesson combination will have you learning to commit to yourself and discover your own self-worth; when you do, you will easily commit to others and accept them too. You are learning to not commit to others in detriment to yourself. You are learning not to be judgemental and critical of others and their commitments. You may be learning to not fear commitment because you feel you or the other person isn't good enough. You are learning not to take things so personally. You are learning that just because people don't commit to your dreams, it doesn't mean they are not committed to you. You are learning to not be selfish or lazy, and that commitments should be balanced. You are learning to not overcommit to gain approval. You are learning to not run away as soon as your emotional buttons are pushed. You are learning that no one is perfect. You are learning to move away from bad behaviour. You are learning that commitment is from within and is not about what you or others are worth. You are learning to not take on the negative opinions of others. You are learning forgiveness and tolerance. You are learning to speak your truth and follow your own commitments and direction, and to allow others their right to do the same. You are learning to not overcommit to others so much that your own health and life suffers. You are learning to not over commit to others so that they don't have to commit for themselves and therefore do not learn responsibility.

The emotional filters, feelings, and behaviours: You feel like nothing you do is ever good enough. You feel like you are being rejected when others don't commit to your direction. You reject others who don't commit to your direction. You use criticism and judgement to feel better about yourself. You overcommit to gain acceptance. You fear commitment because you think people won't think you're good enough. You are too critical and can't find someone good enough to commit to. You're lazy, don't commit to your work or chores, and don't help others. You put up with bad behaviour because you have low self-esteem. You reject people if they don't have the same values or views. You feel like you're always trying to prove yourself. You feel the need to justify what you do, or you make others justify what they do. You take things personally. You don't like sharing, or you share too much. You lose your confidence when your commitments are not going well. You blame others when your commitments are not going well. You overcommit to others so that they don't have to be responsible, which leaves you feeling taken advantage of.

Personal Mantra: I am worthy of love and commitment.

34 = 7

Lessons: Self-worth/Acceptance, Stability/Support, and Trust/Belief

Teaching: This soul lesson combination means that you will discover support and stability from others when you accept and believe in yourself. You are learning to believe in yourself, knowing that you are supported and deserve support. You are learning to believe that others will give to you. You are learning to ask for and accept support from others. You are learning to believe that others will accept and believe in you. You are learning to not withhold love and support from others just because you don't believe in their choices. You are learning to not allow the amount of support or acceptance you get from others to affect your self-belief. You are learning to trust and accept others, realising that not everyone has an ulterior motive. You are learning that it's okay for others to have their own beliefs and to support themselves. You are learning that you're good enough to support others. You are learning you are worthy of the belief others place in you. You are learning to trust in your own values and beliefs and not change them to fit in with others.

Emotional filters, feelings, and behaviours: Your confidence is knocked when you don't get the support you believe you should get. You support others in detriment to yourself or to feel worthy. You only support others when it suits you or you can gain from it. You don't ask for support because you believe you won't get it or it won't be good enough. You don't accept other people if their beliefs are different from your own. Other people's beliefs make you feel unsettled as you question whether yours are right. You don't feel worthy of support. You don't believe you should accept support. You are a martyr who believes you are here to support everyone, which affects your health or life. You feel people will judge and criticise you if you make a mistake or don't support them. You are critical of others if they make mistakes or have different values. You feel others will criticise or judge you if you don't offer the support they want.

Personal Mantra: I am worthy of acceptance, trust, and support.

35 = 8

Lessons: Self-worth/Acceptance, Control/Freedom, and Security/Achievement

Teaching: This soul lesson combination will have you learning that you will manifest your secure future when you release control and feel worthy enough to achieve it. You are learning to create your security from within and to not allow others to knock your confidence or control your direction. You are learning you cannot control others or make them feel unworthy in order to feel more secure or better about yourself. You are learning that allowing others to control your security will rob you of your self-worth. You are learning that freedom doesn't come unless you feel worthy enough to achieve it. You are learning worthiness is not dependent on the amount you achieve or the acceptance of others. You are learning that overachieving should not be used to gain acceptance or praise. You are learning that over achieving cannot be used to control your feelings. You are learning not to use criticism to get others to live up to your high expectations, and to not allow others to use criticism or control to get you to live up to their expectations. You are learning to not let the judgements others have of your achievements make you feel like you need to prove yourself or your worth. You are learning not to allow others complete power over your finances or security or you may be left high and dry.

The emotional filters, feelings, and behaviours: You feel everything you achieve is never good enough. You need things to be perfect before you accept them, or else you feel you can't move forward. You have no self-worth or self-drive to achieve what you would really love to do. You feel others control you and don't allow you your freedom. You compare yourself to others and what they have achieved, and it makes you feel like you're not doing well enough. You feel money is always an issue. You feel that others don't live up to your standards, or that others have too high of expectations of you. You feel that criticism from others stops you from achieving what you would like, or you are critical of others and what they are trying to achieve. You feel you need others to provide your security for you, and you don't believe you could do this for yourself. You keep others away because you fear risking your financial security. You're constantly striving for perfection and abundance. You have lost money, and now you don't trust yourself or your dreams. You feel others are trying to rip you off, and you don't feel secure in your dealings with others. You take things personally.

Personal Mantra: I am worthy of acceptance and the freedom to achieve all my dreams.

36 = 9

Lessons: Self-worth/Acceptance, Commitment/Sharing, and Humility/ Giving and Receiving.

Teaching: This soul lesson combination will have you learning to bring your giving and receiving into balance so that you do not need the acceptance of others to make you feel worthy. You are learning to accept and trust in yourself in order to step into your own personal power with confidence. You will learn that others will commit to you when you feel worthy within yourself and know how to give to both yourself and others in balance. You are learning not to be a martyr and overcommit to everyone else so that your life and health suffers. You are learning that what you receive from others is not a reflection of your own worth. You are learning to not base your self-worth on the amount others show up for you or give to you. You are learning that when you overcommit and help others, you are robbing them of their responsibility and ability to learn. You are learning to not allow others to criticise you and use guilt to get you to give more or commit more to them. You are learning that you cannot use what you do for others as a way to gain their acceptance or commitment. You are learning that you deserve to receive help and can ask for help from others.

The emotional filters and behaviours: You feel you are always giving and that no one is there for you when you need. You feel better about yourself when you are giving to others. You drop everything to be there for others if they need. You overcommit yourself to others, and your own health and well-being are suffering. You feel guilty if you can't be there for others, or others make you feel guilty for not being there for them. You believe it's more important to give than to receive. You try to help others or feel you know what others need, even when you have not been asked to assist. You criticise or reject others if they don't show the same level of commitment you have given to them. You believe everyone should be as giving as you. You take on the responsibilities of others because you don't believe they can do it, or they can't do it as good as you. You are critical of others when they can't do something or don't do something as well as you can. You feel you are not worthy of receiving. You feel that you are the giver, and no one ever gives or commits to you.

Personal Mantra: I am worthy of receiving, and I commit to myself and others equally and in balance.

37 = 10 = 1

Lessons: Self-worth/Acceptance, Trust/Belief, Independence/Abandonment, Codependence/Attention, and Repeated/Not completed

Teaching: This soul lesson combination will have you learning and discovering the importance of your belief and acceptance of self, as well as radiating your inner power. It is important that you understand, accept, and believe in your own values. Follow your own direction without the need to rely on external sources to validate you or give you confidence.

You may find it difficult to accept and believe in yourself, stand in your own power, and stand up for your own rights and values. Alternatively, you may force your beliefs, values, and opinions on others. You are learning that other people's acceptance and judgement of you is not a reason to doubt yourself. You are learning that you can't be overly critical and abandon others who don't have the same beliefs and values as you. You are learning to not abandon your own beliefs and values for others because you feel less worthy than them. You are learning you don't need the belief and acceptance of others to believe in and accept yourself. You are learning not to be a martyr and abandon yourself for everyone else because you believe others are worthier than you. You are learning you don't need to be saintly or perfect for fear that others will criticise or not accept you if you make a mistake. You are learning you are perfectly imperfect. You have nothing to prove to yourself or others in order to validate your worthiness or your beliefs.

The emotional filters, feelings, and behaviours: You abandon yourself, your beliefs, or your values for others or to keep others happy. You are emotionally needy or rely heavily on others to make you feel good about yourself or to validate your self-belief. You are opinionated and don't listen to others or tolerate other people's different beliefs. You feel like you are not accepted or listened to. You are emotionally distant or detached from others for fear of being let down or hurt. You need your feelings validated by others. You believe others should make you happy by accepting you and your values. You are critical of others. You use addictive or codependent behaviour to feel better or give you self-confidence. You give your heart too easily, or you don't let in others. You believe there is no one for you because no one can live up to your high standards. You don't believe you are good enough, and you constantly sabotage yourself. You believe in others too much and don't trust your instincts, only to be let down. You undersell your own values so that others like and accept you, or to keep them happy. You allow or put up with codependent behaviour for fear of being abandoned.

Personal Mantra: I am confident and self-assured, and I believe I can stand in my own power with acceptance and grace.

38 = 11 = 2

Lessons: Self-worth/Acceptance, Security/Achievement, Independence/Abandonment, and Codependence/Attention

Teaching: This soul lesson combination will have you learning to not abandon yourself and your dreams because of others or because of your own lack of confidence or self-worth. You are learning to feel secure in your own right and to not rely on others for your sense of achievement. You are also learning that you can't help others with their own security in order to help you feel better about yourself or prove your worth to them. You are learning to not abandon your own values for others because you feel more secure when you go with the status quo. You are learning to not abandon others when they don't meet your high expectations. You are learning that security and achievement will come when you feel you are worthy of it and follow your own inner calling. You are learning to not rely on external validation that you are good enough and are doing well enough. You are learning to not be critical of others and abandon them because of their financial status. You are learning to not use money and security as a way to feel better about yourself or your life. You are learning you cannot rescue others financially because you rob them of their responsibility and ability to learn. You are learning that you can't be rescued financially without it affecting your own worth and growth. You are learning you have nothing to prove to others or yourself. You are learning to speak your truth without being opinionated.

The emotional filters, feelings, and behaviours: You don't feel good enough in your achievements. You will only feel good enough when you achieve financial success. You abandon your achievements to help others with theirs due to a lack of belief and confidence in your own. You give to everyone else to the detriment of yourself, and your own financial security suffers. You only feel good enough or that you're doing well enough when you get external validation or praise from others. If others don't accept your ideas and your direction, you lose confidence in yourself. You are critical of others who don't meet your high expectations or do things as well as you. You reject others and do things yourself because they don't do it as well as you can. You don't speak up for yourself at work, or you speak your mind too much. You compare yourself to the success and security others have, and it makes you feel you aren't doing well enough. You reject or accept others based on their financial status. You feel others reject or accept you based on your financial status. You abandon your dreams because you don't feel you can achieve them or are unworthy of success. You fear success and achievement. You rely on others for financial support because you don't believe you can achieve it in your own right.

Personal Mantra: I am worthy of achieving all my dreams and desires.

39 = 12 = 3

Lessons: Self-worth/Acceptance, Humility/Giving and Receiving, Independence/Abandonment, and Codependence/Attention

Teaching: This soul lesson combination will have you learning that you can't use giving and receiving as a way to feel good about yourself. You are learning to bring your giving and receiving back into balance, especially if you don't know how to receive. You are learning to not abandon yourself to be there for everyone else. You are learning that your self-worth or external validation doesn't come from you being a martyr. You are learning that you can't judge the amount others give you as evidence of how much they accept or like you. You are learning to not give to others when they don't request it, even if you feel they need it. You are learning that by giving too much to others, you are robbing them of their responsibility to learn to do things for themselves. You are learning that when you don't receive from others, it is not a reflection of your worthiness. You don't need validation and acceptance from others in order to feel good about yourself. You are learning to not be critical of or reject others simply because they don't give you what you want or what you were expecting. You are learning to not use giving as a way of receiving positive attention. You are learning that when you don't receive positive praise and acceptance from others, this doesn't mean you are unworthy. You are learning to not take things so personally.

The emotional filters, feelings, and behaviours: You feel that whatever you do is not good enough, or that others are judging you as not good enough. You take things personally. You feel better when you are giving to others and abandon yourself and your own needs. You let yourself or others down because you do things out of obligation and find it difficult to say no. You accept the opinions of others and give too much attention to them. You fear making a mistake, and so you find it hard to make decisions because you don't want to be criticised. You give too much to others, and they rely too heavily on you. You fear others will abandon you if you don't give to them. You give too much to others and try to help them because you feel you know better and they can't help themselves. You are critical of others who don't give enough or do enough for you. You feel you are always the giver and never the receiver. You find it difficult to accept compliments or receive from others. When you see that others have received more than you, it makes you feel rejected or unworthy. You find it difficult to praise others, or you don't feel like you get any praise. You need a lot of attention or external validation in order to feel good about yourself and your life. You give a lot of validation and praise to others so that they like you and accept you.

Personal Mantra: I am worthy of receiving love and attention from myself and others.

40 = 4

Lessons: Stability/Support and Repeated/Not completed

Teaching: If you have this lesson, you must understand that when you learn to find the balance between asking for support and accepting support, then others will be more supportive of you.

The emotional filters, feelings and behaviours: You feel unsupported by others. You don't support others. You find it difficult to ask for and accept support. You support others in detriment to yourself. You feel that if you don't support others, their world or your world would fall apart. You feel that you don't get enough help. You don't ask for help. You expect others should know what you need. You feel like no one is ever there for you. You support others so much that your own life and health suffers.

Personal Mantra: I am loved and supported in all that I do.

41 = 5

Lessons: Stability/Support, Independence/Abandonment, Codependence/ Attention, and Control/Freedom

Teaching: This soul lesson combination will have you learning that you cannot find support and attention through manipulating and controlling others, or by allowing yourself to be manipulated or controlled. You will learn that being yourself and allowing both yourself and others the freedom to experience life will result in the support and validation you seek. You will also learn to stand in your power and not allow the opinions and judgement of others to control the way you support and treat yourself. You may need to learn that others won't always abandon you if you don't offer the support they want. You are learning to not use the support you give to others as a way to feel more loved. You are learning to not use the amount of support you receive from others as a measure of their love. You are learning you should not abandon yourself for everyone else. You are learning that manipulation can't be used to get the outcome you want. You are learning you have no control over the behaviour of others and are not responsible for fixing others.

The emotional filters, feelings, and behaviours: You feel like you have no control over the support you get from others. You feel like others emotionally control you to give them support. You feel like you're abandoned by others when they don't support you. You abandon others when they need support. You fear standing up for yourself and asking for support. You feel others will think you are not in control of your own life if you ask for help. You overly support others to validate yourself or because you fear abandonment. You abandon yourself and your goals to support others. You feel like your need for support is rejected by others unless it suits them. You give support to manipulate or control others to get what you want. You fear if you don't give others support, they won't love you or will abandon you.

Personal Mantra: I am lovingly supported and free to be me.

42 = 6

Lessons: Stability/Support, Codependence/Attention, Independence/Abandonment, and Commitment/Sharing

Teaching: This soul lesson combination is learning that you have a voice and deserve the commitment and support of others. You are also learning the importance of committing to yourself and finding your own stability from within, especially in any areas you have let go. You are learning that commitments should be balanced with equal support of both self and others. You are learning to not overcommit yourself and abandon your own life for everyone else. You may be using overcommitting to others to gain attention or validation from them. You are learning to not seek constant reassurance from others in order to feel stable. You are learning that if people don't give you the support and attention you think you need, it doesn't always mean they are not committed or are going to abandon you. You are learning to not oversupport or overcommit to others because they won't learn how to be responsible for themselves.

The emotional filters, feelings, and behaviours: You feel unsupported by others through their lack of commitment. You abandon your own commitments to support others because you fear standing up for yourself. You overcommit or oversupport others to gain attention. You undercommit due to feeling overwhelmed or a lack of self-support. You stay in a relationship or job for fear of letting others down. If people are not giving you the support you need, you question their commitment to you. You commit quickly and lose your sense of self to those who give you positive attention or love. You have no freedom or time because you're too busy fixing everyone else. You feel you need to be there for everyone. You don't feel stable unless others validate their commitment to you. You oversupport others and believe if you don't, their world will fall apart. You live your life through the support and commitment to others.

Personal Mantra: I am committed to lovingly supporting myself and others in balance.

43 = 7

Lessons: Support/Stability, Self-worth/Acceptance, and Trust/Belief

Teaching: This soul lesson combination will let you discover support and stability from others when you accept and believe in yourself. You are learning to believe in yourself because you are supported and deserve support. You are learning to believe that others will give to you. You are learning to ask for and accept support from others. You are learning to believe that others will accept and believe in you. You are learning to not withhold love and support from others just because you don't believe in their choices. You are learning to not allow the amount of support or acceptance you get from others to affect your self-belief. You are learning to trust and accept others, because not everyone has an ulterior motive. You are learning that it's okay for others to have their own beliefs and to support themselves. You are learning that you're good enough to support others. You are learning you are worthy of the belief others place in you. You are learning to trust in your own values and beliefs, and to not change them to fit in with others.

Emotional filters, feelings, and behaviours: Your confidence is knocked when you don't get the support you believe you should get. You support others in detriment to yourself or to make yourself feel worthy. You only support others when it suits you or you can gain from it. You don't ask for support because you believe you won't get it or it won't be good enough. You don't accept other people if their beliefs are different from your own. Other people's beliefs make you feel unsettled as you question whether yours are right. You don't feel worthy of support. You don't believe you should accept support. You are a martyr who believes you are here to support everyone, which affects your health or life. You feel people will judge and criticise you if you make a mistake or don't support them. You are critical of others if they make a mistake or have different values. You feel others will criticise or judge you if you don't offer the support they want.

Personal Mantra: I am worthy of acceptance, trust, and support.

44 = 8

Lessons: Stability/Support and Security/Achievement

Teaching: This soul lesson combination will have you learning to keep the support of self and others in balance in order to feel secure and achieve your dreams. You are learning that you can't oversupport others, or else your own achievements and security will suffer. You are learning that you need the help and support of others in order to fulfil your own achievements. You are learning to not rely on the support of others in order to feel secure in what you are doing. You are learning the importance of work-family balance and that success is not a substitute for emotional connection. You are learning to not give up on your own dreams and goals in order to support the needs of others. You are learning that perfection and high expectation are not everyone's values. You are learning that you can ask for help, and it is not a sign of failure. You are learning to support yourself, and if you rely too heavily on others to support you, you will lose your sense of security.

The emotional filters, feelings, and behaviours: You feel you must support everyone else, but you don't get support in return. You don't know how to ask for or receive support from others. You have high expectations of yourself and others, and you don't feel supported by others when they don't live up to your expectations. You overly support others so that they feel secure to the detriment of your own security and achievements. You are too supportive of others, to the point that your own work suffers. You use the amount of support you receive as a measure of how well you are achieving. You don't support yourself enough to achieve your own security, or you rely heavily on others to provide your security. You have high expectations of yourself and others, and you don't feel secure unless you achieve these high expectations.

Personal Mantra: I am supporting myself and others in balance to attract and achieve all of my desires.

45 = 9

Lessons: Stability/Support, Control/Freedom, and Humility/Giving and Receiving

Teaching: This soul lesson combination will have you learning that you will gain your sense of freedom when you bring your giving and support to others into balance. You are learning that you cannot use support or giving to gain something in return. You are learning to not give in detriment to yourself, and it's okay to give to yourself. You are learning to not support in detriment to yourself, and to support yourself in balance. You are learning to receive support and to ask for what you want and need. You are learning that giving too much to others or overly supporting them is not helping them learn their own responsibilities. You are learning to not allow others to control you with their demands for support. You are learning to go with the flow and to not have such high expectations of yourself and others. You are learning you can't control the amount of support you get or expect from others. You are learning you can only control your own life, and in order to move forward, sometimes you need to surrender and go with the flow. You are learning to step outside of your comfort zone.

The emotional filters, feelings, and behaviours: You don't know how to say no. You feel unsupported when others say no or don't give you support. You feel you are always the one doing the supporting or giving to others. You spend too much time giving to everyone else, and you don't have time for you. You give to others and support others too much, thus robbing them of their own responsibilities and the ability to learn and grow. Others manipulate you into supporting and giving to them. You don't ask for support or help from others. You are going with the flow too much and don't support yourself with what you need to do. You are a control freak and don't allow others to help you or support you. You control others so much that they don't know how to support themselves. You feel it's always better to give than to receive, and then you find you never have enough for you. You feel like everyone wants you to make them happy. You feel like others should be making you happy.

Mantra: I am going with the flow of life, and I gratefully give and receive love and support.

46 = 10 = 1

Lessons: Stability/Support, Commitment/Sharing, Independence/Abandonment, Codependence/Attention, and Repeated/Not Completed

Teaching: This soul lesson combination will have you learning to value yourself by keeping your support and commitment to yourself in balance. You are learning that you deserve to be supported and don't always have to be the strong one. You will learn others will commit to you and support you. You are learning to not dishonour your own commitments and values by abandoning them for everyone else. You are learning to not overcommit to others and abandon yourself. You are learning that when you overly support others, you are not allowing them to learn their responsibilities. When you allow others to overly support you, you are not learning your responsibility. You are learning that not everyone has the same values as you. You are learning to stand in your power and stand up for your own values, but you don't have to force them on others. You are learning that you don't need to validate yourself through external sources or through the amount of support or commitment you receive or don't receive. You are learning to not overcommit to supporting others because you will lose yourself. You are learning to not shut down others or reject them when you feel their support and commitment is not up to your standard.

The emotional filters, feelings, and behaviours: You overcommit to supporting everyone around you, and you suffer because of it. You feel like people don't follow through and do what they say, and they are never there for you when you need. You don't follow through with your own commitments because you are too busy helping others. You expect others to help you and be there for you. You support others even when it's not asked for. You reject others who let you down and don't support you in the way you think they should. You feel others are selfish when they don't consider you. You feel selfish if you don't put others before you. You live through your family and are at their beck and call. You do your own thing regardless of others. You don't connect to others for fear of being let down. You have high expectations of others and withdraw your commitment to them if they don't live up to these standards. You keep supporting others even when you know it's not good for them or you. You fear that if you don't give others the support they want from you, they will abandon you. You can't understand why people won't commit to you when you are such a supportive person towards them.

Personal Mantra: I am appreciated and committed to supporting myself and others in balance.

47 = 11 = 2

Lessons: Stability/Support, Trust/Belief, Independence/Abandonment, and Codependence/Attention

Teaching: This soul lesson combination will have you learning to believe that you deserve to be acknowledged and supported. You will learn to believe in yourself and stand in your own power, but you should not force your beliefs and values on others. You will learn to ask for support and believe that you will receive it. You are learning to not support others in detriment to yourself or out of obligation. You are learning to trust that others don't always have an ulterior motive or are going to let you down. You are learning to trust and believe in yourself. You are learning to believe that you can support yourself and your dreams. You are learning that you don't need to rely on external sources to support you or your vision. You are learning that others have their own values, and when they don't match yours, you don't have to abandon your beliefs or force your beliefs on them. You are learning to not overly support those who don't believe in themselves, or else you are robbing them of an opportunity to grow. You are learning not to be a martyr through oversupporting others.

The emotional filters, feelings, and behaviours: You don't believe you can support yourself or believe in your dreams. You feel others don't believe in you or support your values and beliefs. You support others at a cost to yourself, and you don't believe anyone supports you. You feel you need the support of others to make decisions. You don't trust others and feel others are trying to get something from you, or they are going to let you down. You feel abandoned when you don't get the support you expected. You use support as a way to gain people's trust and validation. You overly support others because you believe you are helping them and they can't help themselves. You overly support others and believe you will be abandoned if you don't. You have trust issues and look for evidence that a person is trustworthy. You are not trustworthy and look for external validation through things you believe will make you happier. You take life too seriously or feel the need to be saintly because you don't wish to let down anyone.

Personal Mantra: I am self-assured and supported in my self-belief.

48 = 12 = 3

Lessons: Stability/Support, Security/Achievement, Independence/Abandonment, Codependence/Attention, and Self-worth/Acceptance

Teaching: This soul lesson combination will have you learning you are good enough to receive the support you need to achieve your dreams. You are learning you are worthy of support and can ask for the support you need. You are learning to not abandon yourself by overly supporting others and their achievements. You are learning that you will lose your self-confidence if you rely heavily on others to support you and provide your security. You will learn that security comes when you value yourself enough to accept you are worthy of achievement. You are learning that you have your own values and opinions, but you shouldn't force them on others, and they shouldn't force theirs on you. You are learning that when you overly support others, you are robbing them of their own achievements. You are learning to stand in your own power and say no with confidence. You are learning you are worthy, valued, and accepted, and you don't need external sources to validate this. You are learning to achieve work-life balance, and you can't use security and achievement as a substitute for emotional connection. You are learning that you will never be good enough while you are trying to prove you are.

The emotional filters, feelings, and behaviours: You feel you are not good enough to follow your own direction and dreams. You feel others don't support your achievements and dreams. You feel you need to prove yourself. You feel what you have achieved is still not good enough. You have high expectations of yourself and lose your confidence when you don't achieve them. You have high expectations of others and feel unsupported and critical of them if they don't live up to these expectations. You don't accept flaws; you like perfection and are always striving for the best. You feel you won't be accepted or will be judged by others if you don't achieve your goals. You feel others will abandon you, judge you, or reject you if you don't give them the security and support they want. You abandon yourself while trying to support others to ensure they feel secure. You rely on others to support you and make you feel secure. You use money and things to gain attention, which helps you feel more worthy and secure. You use external sources to give you confidence and to make you feel accepted and secure. You criticise and reject others when you don't get the support or attention you wanted. You judge and criticise people who have less than you or more than you. You feel more comfortable supporting your family through achievement than emotional connection.

Personal Mantra: I am worthy of love and support, and I am confident I can achieve my dreams.

Review

You now know that your soul lessons were set up in your childhood, and that your past relationship issues and failures are just the teachings of these soul lessons. You know that when your emotional buttons are being pushed, your soul lessons are in reaction. As you have worked your way through this chapter, you will have discovered your own personal blueprint and profile, identifying the feelings and behaviours your ego presents with and perceives situations through.

Now you're ready to take this knowledge deeper and use it to help you understand and expose these patterns in your everyday life. Knowing how you perceive through these soul lessons is a giant leap forward in awakening, but we still have much deeper to go in order to understand the part you play in attracting and creating these soul lesson patterns. Every situation that has happened to you, or that you have ever experienced, has one common denominator, and that is you. This happened to you for the purpose of growth, and the situation had what you were learning jumping out at you the whole time.

Let's go do some very deep work. For some, this may push buttons. I'm not here to fluff around the edges and jump on the pity plane with you. Most of us have had some pretty bad stuff happen to us in our lives, and it's time to heal, get the lesson, empower ourselves, and move on up to a much better place. To do that, we make it our purpose to be responsible for the part of us that attracted it or created it. Focus only on your part. The other parties will have to deal with their own parts and karma. For you to move forward, you will need to be responsible for yourself, because you have no control over others and their behaviour.

If you're feeling empowered and brave enough to take on your ego on, I'll see you in the next chapter.

My Life Has Evolved
by Lea-Anne Lavelle

People come into our lives for a reason, and at first I didn't realize how big an impact on my life Julie would have. Looking back, especially over the last four years, my life has evolved with Julie's help.

Before doing the Love Life Retreat Programme, I was my own worst enemy. I had too high expectations of not only myself but others. I always reacted when people pushed my buttons. My closest friends commented on how I would put up a barrier if anybody got too close. I couldn't see this, let alone know the reason why or how to overcome it. I often found myself looking for acceptance and reassurance from others, wanting something to fulfil me. I was very independent and found it difficult to ask for and accept help. But on the other hand, I had no problem giving help to others because it was always a wonderful feeling.

I have come to know and have understanding of my soul lessons and with Julie's wonderful teaching and guidance, I have been able to remove the old emotional blocks, heal, and move forward. When my buttons are pushed now, I realise it is my soul lessons that are in reaction.

Meditation has helped still my mind, given me a feeling of balance, and opened my heart to receive love, give love, and listen to my higher self for guidance whenever I become aware of something that needs to heal.

By honouring and loving my body, mind, and spirit, I feel that I can experience the most amazing relationship with myself, and this in turn is reflected in others.

CHAPTER 6

Unpacking and Reflecting

> By three methods we may learn wisdom: First, by
> reflection, which is noblest; Second, by imitation, which
> is easiest; and third by experience, which is the bitterest.
> —Confucius

It's awesome that you are feeling brave and are ready to face your stuff. This work is going to help you uncover the beliefs and behaviours that we don't often see but have a massive effect on our perceptions and actions. It's because we don't know they are there that we keep repeating cycle after cycle of emotional pain.

The hardest thing you are ever going to do in this lifetime is to free yourself from your own ego and its limiting beliefs and emotional filters. If this was easy, everyone would be thinking positive and creating the lives of their dreams. There are a lot of people for whom this is not possible at this moment, because these limiting beliefs and emotional patterns are holding them stuck. I am sure you have heard or read that all you need to do is keep your thoughts and vibration in joy and positivity, and you will attract all you need. That's right, you will. But for a lot of people, telling them to keep their thoughts positive when their inner and outer worlds are full of emotional turmoil is like handing them a degree when they haven't completed the study. They might be able to wing it for a while, but then it becomes all too hard, and they will only revert back to the level they have learnt and know.

I believe you need to understand your inner world first, or else you will have difficulty changing the outside world it is creating. I know this because I had to learn this too, and because you are here with me now, I am guessing you do too. I want to give you a confidence boost by letting you know that you already have everything within you to change your life and live the life of your dreams. You simply have to uncover and heal it to set your spirit free.

You can do this, because I did it. I used to be an insecure drama queen with absolutely no self-confidence at all, and I wanted to give up on life a few times in my younger days. If I can do this, so can you. Your spirit has guided you here, and you have made it this far. I admire your courage, so good on you!

Now, it's time for some tough love,

It's time to show all our excuses and justifications the door, and expose our inner stuff for what it truly is, because, excuses, justifications, blame, and judgement are giving our pain a reason to exist! They are all symptoms of a stuck, stubborn, uninspired, and lazy ego. Change does not happen by sitting in our stuff.

Today you may feel good, but tomorrow you may feel like crap, and that's when the ego is likely to kick in with its BS and its desire to give up, because you think it's too hard or you can't do it. The minute you tell yourself you can't do something, your ego has sold you out, and you will create this as your reality and remain stuck. Remember that you have another side to you, your spirit, and it wants to shine.

Healing is a journey and a practise, not an instant fix. It is a journey you start. You fall down, you get back up, you dust yourself off, and you learn something. You keep going and keep moving forward, and when you're moving forward, you are growing and evolving. Then one day, you will look back, give yourself a fancy high-five, and say, "Wow, look how far I've come." Then wham—the next learning appears because you're ready to grow again. But this time, you are armed and ready to face this sucker head-on, because you have grown and evolved and are more experienced and empowered this next time around. This is life—real life!

No more justifying or excuses. It will take effort, and it will mean you will have to dig deep and make some changes. You matter, and you're worth making these changes for, so this is not being selfish. It called being centred in self, and there's a huge difference.

Now that you have discovered your personal soul lessons via the relationship blueprint and profile and your emotional filters, it's time to expose the old emotional patterns your soul lessons have created, and to uncover the hidden stuff.

This chapter will help you expose and unpack your soul lessons so you can understand what changes are needed in order to move forward. You are not just unpacking your soul lessons here; you are unpacking the real you, the you who is hidden behind your stuff.

Being brave is all about understanding the part we play in our stuff. That's the last thing people who have gone from one relationship disaster to another want to hear. They are usually too busy reacting and focusing on what others have put them through, as well as the injustice of everything that has been done to them. They can't see the part they play in a situation if they continue to use blame and judgement and focus on the pain instead of healing it.

Here is the deal. If this is you, I am not saying you are to blame, because every situation with another person contains mutual learning. You both are playing a part in it, and if there was nothing to learn, you wouldn't have experienced it. There was a reason you accepted this relationship and got into it in the first place, and that part needs healing. Either this person was always a jerk but you chose not to see it, or the person turned into one because you pushed his buttons and reflected something in him that he couldn't handle. It doesn't matter, and he no longer matters. What does matter is that you are ready to own your part and look deeply into why this showed up for you and what you are were meant to learn from this experience—and every experience where your buttons are pushed.

Next, I am going to share with you the four key steps to understanding how to unpack your soul lessons. To start off at step one, you use something that is ticking you off and pushing your buttons. If you are feeling pretty good right now, that's awesome; you will simply have to wait until someone comes along and pushes your buttons, and then you will have your starting point. We have lots of soul teachers around us who know exactly what we need to learn; they are masters at knowing which buttons to push, so you probably won't have to wait too long. At some point, someone will oblige and cause an emotional reaction within you. If you want to work on something that has happened in the past, you can use that as your starting point. Once you have your reaction, it's time to learn to chuck a hissy fit with purpose.

Step 1: Hissy Fit with Purpose

Yes, it's okay to be angry or sad, and to let your negative emotions flow. If you don't let them out, they will still show up through your ego and create more blocks that continue to build up until you explode or fall down in a depressed heap because you have held onto your stuff for so long. It is normal to feel grumpy, overwhelmed, angry, and frustrated; even highly evolved people get the shits sometimes and want to tell the world and others to shove off. The difference is they don't react and reflect this onto others; instead, they own it and work within to regain their balance and evolve.

Your emotional reaction and hissy fit is going to contain the clues to whatever it is you are not seeing and longing to change, heal, and evolve within you so that you can move forward out of any emotional patterns that are keeping you stuck. Grab a journal, some paper, or the back of the Wheaties box if you have to. Write it out. Write out exactly how you feel, how someone else is making you feel. Include your judgements and perception of the situation, and yes, for this step you can blame, jump up and down, and cry at the injustice of it all. Simply write it all down and get it out, because your thoughts are always going to be worse in your mind. You will find it easier to expose your lessons when they're written down in front of you and not simply doing loops in your mind.

If you have done a lot of inner work prior to reading this book, then you will understand the strength of the ego when it has a hissy fit and throws you off balance. Every now and again, we get a good one, and because we've already done loads of work on ourselves, we can get frustrated to see more appear. Sometimes we even get a doozy that has us falling back into bad habits. Then when we have bashed our heads against the brick wall for a bit, we regain our composure and get back to our spirit because we have learnt that the only way forward is to jump back onto the self-evolving wagon. There is not much that pushes my buttons these days, but when it does, it's usually a big one. Yes, I am human and have an ego too.

Step 2: Find Your Balance

You are not going to be able to do the inner work required if you are in emotional turmoil. Your mind will overpower you and quite often keep the situation going around and around in your head. Finding your balance as the yin-yang symbol suggests is paramount to moving forward. This is going to be different for everyone, and everyone will differ in the amount of time it takes to do so. Finding your balance means being able to ground and recentre yourself with calmness by quietening and redirecting the mind and calming the emotional reaction. For some, it may be as easy as telling your mind to sit down and shut the hell up, because it's not helping you. For others, it will be a combination of things. Here are my suggestions to reconnect you to your balance. Try them and then use the ones that feel right for you. The most important part of this step is to understand that it will be difficult to move forward unless you find your balance first.

Wisdom Note: Finding your balance can be difficult when you are going through a loss or something traumatic. Sometimes you will have to allow yourself the time it takes for you to go through a perfectly natural emotional process like grief. It's okay to feel sad, lonely fearful, hurt, anxious, and all the emotions we are here to experience. Get comfortable with your feelings, and get comfortable with asking for support and help when you need. You will know when you're ready to move forward and find your balance, because you'll have had enough of feeling these negative emotions, and you'll feel ready. We don't want to get stuck in these emotions for years; we want to deal with them as soon as we can. Sometimes you need to be kind to yourself and let yourself feel your emotions. You will know when you have had enough and are ready to move forward until them accept your feelings.

Julie Kay

Journal

Writing it out gets your thoughts out of your mind and onto paper. That is a great way to bring your mind into balance. Through the pop-up, feel-good shop, I have designed a positively focused journal. It contains a daily exercise, positive quotes, and pages of inspiration to help keep you on track to being positively focused. Get one, or use an old notebook; it doesn't matter. It is a wonderful exercise to help you become more aware of how you feel and what you think about your life. A bonus to journaling that you may not have previously considered is you will witness your own evolvement. When you go back and read your past journals, you will see through your own words how far you have come and how much you have grown.

Meditate

Meditation is a well-known modality for bringing harmony and balance to the mind. That's why many psychologists and doctors recommend this as a therapeutic practise. If you struggle with meditation, start with a guided one that is no longer than ten to fifteen minutes. Your mind can then focus on the leader's voice, which will give it something to do. Practise is required, so don't give up. When I first tried meditation back in the early nineties, I thought there was no way I was ever going to be able to do it. I persevered and learnt. Meditation does not require you to sit like a Zen monk and not think at all. Not thinking is virtually impossible. It teaches you to slow down and redirect your thoughts to calmness and balance.

Although not thinking is virtually impossible, here is a little game I like to teach some of my clients, to show them that they can stop their minds in their tracks, which is the first step to learning to redirect it. Try to stop your thoughts and see how long you can do this for. Then when a thought pops in, stop it again and see if you can go for longer. Try this for one minute and see how you go. See if you can hold your mind blank for longer than a just a few seconds. If you can stop your mind in this exercise, you can take control of it and redirect it. You do have the power to take control of your mind and put it back in its box, instead of it controlling you. It simply takes practice, patience, and perseverance.

Breathing

Long, slow, deep breaths have a calming effect on your body and allow you to centre and balance. Slow, deep breathing regulates the oxygen and carbon dioxide levels in your bloodstream. When you are anxious, your breathing is shallow and fast. This places these levels out of balance, and the physiological systems of the body, including the brain, cannot function as effectively.

Take a nice deep breath in for four counts, hold for four counts, and then breathe out for four counts. Repeat this four times. This can have an instant calming effect.

Read

Grab an inspirational non-fiction book. Nothing inspires the intellectual ego more than giving it something to learn. The physical side of self is the learning side, and it's what it does best. Learn more about you and the ways you can evolve what you love. You are doing it right now. Doesn't if feel better to learn?

Exercise

This is a great way to bring you back into balance and tire out the mind. Go for a walk or do something vigorous. You will release endorphins that make you feel better and more balanced.

Low energy can go hand in hand with a low emotional state. To ramp up your energy, you create more energy. Think of a ball rolling down a hill. As it does it gathers momentum, the more energy it creates, the faster it goes. Sitting on the couch and thinking about your woes is not creating momentum or bringing you into balance. Get out there and ramp up your energy and good feelings with movement and exercise.

Sit in Nature

I don't think there are very many people who would say nature makes them feel stressed, unless you come across a big spider or snake while out there. Mother Earth is abundant with beauty, and you simply have to go find some and soak up the energy. The ocean is particularly good for bringing you back to balance. The sun shining down on the ocean releases negative ions in the evaporation process, and these are good for your energy. They discharge the positive ions that drain us from the electromagnetic radiation that comes from computers, artificial lighting, and TV.

Diet

What we feed and water our bodies, we are feeding our minds. What you are putting in is either robbing you of energy or giving you energy. I don't need to nag you about this. I am sure you are already nagging yourself if this is out of balance.

Create a Relaxing Space

There is nothing more relaxing than a bath set in the ambience of relaxation music and candles. Mix in some salt and essential oils, and there's my heaven.

Whatever works for you to bring you back into a grounded, balanced state of well-being, do it as soon as possible. Have your hissy fit and then find your balance so that you can move into the next step of exposing and unpacking your lessons. These next two steps are quite intense, especially while you are learning. If it gets a bit too much, have a break and revisit. Read them over and over until you completely understand them.

Wisdom Note: If you are struggling with finding your balance, then get some help. You never have to struggle alone. See a counsellor, life coach, spiritual profiler, or healer—whatever aligns to you. Remember that it will be hard to for you to move forward if you are in emotional turmoil and reaction.

Step 3: Self-reflection

Let's rehash. You now know your lessons, how they were set up, how to have a hissy fit with purpose, and how to find your balance. Now it's time to dig out what you're learning. Your lessons will always be present, however the situation and circumstances that push your emotional buttons can show up within different scenarios. I mentioned earlier that the reason you have a hissy fit with purpose is to help you see what it is you are currently not seeing, because you will find the gem of wisdom in your own emotional reaction.

Judgement, blame, justifications, and excuses are simply giving your pain a reason to exist, and they're also telling you what you have been missing.

The key to what you are not seeing is always within the judgement. We are constantly judging everything in our lives as good or bad all the time. We live in the world of duality, and so that's how we do it here on the earth plane; it's normal human behaviour. When you're consciously connected, you start to realise that nothing really is good or bad, it just is, and our perception of the situation makes it one or the other. You might think something is really good, and another person perceives it as really bad, so it is both good and bad in the bigger picture. It comes down to morals, values, and perception.

The universe or God consciousness is also good and bad. Within this consciousness, we have love and hate and both make up the whole. Even in the spirit realms, there is the lower vibrational realm called the astral plane, and then other realms that range up in vibration to the master realm. They are all connected and part of each other in what we call the God consciousness. Good and bad coexist, especially here on the earth plane, where our physical bodies give us the law of duality in the physical, intellectual, and emotional sense.

Nothing is really good or bad in the bigger picture; it is only your perception of it that will make it so. It's okay for us to have healthy, balanced judgements; they help us set our internal morals and values compass, which we can use as a comparison tool to ensure we are moving forward and growing. It can also allow us to determine who and what we are in alignment with.

Judgement can be helpful or harmful—there's that duality again. It is harmful when it is bringing up our soul lessons, giving us emotional reactions and instability, and causing cycles of issues and pain in our lives.

Have you ever had an experience where someone was judging you or blaming you for something, and you thought to yourself, "That's sounds more like you than me"? I would always know when one of my partners was not meeting his budget at work, because he would come home and have a go at me about money and how much I was earning and spending.

I believe we can't see something in someone else that is not part of us, even the really bad stuff. There is always an element of you in your judgements for them to exist, or you wouldn't be able to see the judgement in the first place. I also believe the severity of the emotional reaction is in direct balance to how much you are not seeing it within you; the more intense the reaction, the deeper it is. Stay with me here, and I promise it will make sense.

This is a bit tricky to understand, because although the experience that triggered the judgement may not be exactly the same, there is still something this experience is triggering and bringing up in you. If you are not seeing it in your life, then you will see it in others. What you are about to learn is that we are never as ticked off by others as much as we are internally ticked off with ourselves.

We have to go deep here, and so I am going to use an example that will shock most people to help you understand where I am coming from. Of course, not all reflections are going to be as deep as my example. I feel if I start with something challenging, then it will be easier for you to recognise the less challenging ones. Please note that this work *does not* condone bad behaviour. Bad behaviour is bad behaviour, and people still need to be responsible for the consequences of their choices. What we are determining is why something can trigger an emotional reaction within you.

I will be tackling a subject that is very sensitive to a lot of people, so if you have experienced any kind of abuse in your past, I ask you to consider your mental and emotional health before you read on. You may want to go through this section with your support person or counsellor if you feel that reading and self-reflection on this subject may cause you emotional or mental harm. You can continue the training after the section surrounded with asterisks, where I have used less emotional reflections.

Read on only if you are able to take full responsibility for your life and your emotional and mental health.

The reason I am using such a deeply emotional experience as an example is because I want you to see that regardless of what is being triggered on the outside, it's also happening on the inside. If you don't change the emotional trigger on the inside, then you will continue to experience it. In my book *Soul Lessons to Soul Mate*, I talked about my own childhood experience of sexual abuse. I had worked on this in earlier years, but I never realised the depth of its affect until I found the trigger in my own life. Although I was lucky enough for the abuse to only ever have happened once, the effects showed up in my relationships for many years to come. Only when I healed my internal emotional trigger did the relationships change, and I stopped experiencing the emotional turmoil. Simply because I was no longer being abused, that didn't mean I was no longer abusing myself.

This is powerful stuff.

Let's use an example that will disgust most people: paedophiles. The majority will have a judgement about them as being disgusting human beings who prey on and take advantage of innocent children. For one group of people, that judgement may be more of an observation, and therefore it doesn't have much emotion attached to it. It's simply an opinion based on their personal values, perceptions, and beliefs. However, for another group, that judgement may be laced with an intense emotional reaction that makes them want to react and lash out at paedophiles. Just hearing about one can bring up anger and reaction. Both groups of people think paedophiles are disgusting human beings who prey on innocent children, so why does it affect some emotionally more than others? It is because those who have an intense emotional reaction have something buried deep inside that needs to heal. What that is can be found in the judgement and soul lessons. The judgement now becomes the reflection.

Let's use the group who had the intense emotional reaction as our example. They are disgusted at paedophiles for taking advantage of innocent children; this is the reflection. This judgement and reflection is the key to what these people's own triggers are and what we are looking for within them—what is causing this person to have an intense emotional reaction.

Now, put the paedophiles to the side; they don't have anything to do with this inner process other than to bring the emotional reaction and lesson to our attention.

Once we have the emotional judgement, we can look for the key general points in the judgement. For our example, we could say these key judgements are disgust, being taken advantage of, and innocence. These are the key points that this group would need to reflect back onto themselves to find where they are in them. The behaviour of the paedophile is not what we are looking for. These people are enraged by paedophiles and disgusted by their behaviour, and so they are very unlikely to be one.

It's the emotional key points of our judgements that we are reflecting back to us and looking for in us. This is the hidden emotional pattern you are not aware of, which is why an experience will give you an emotional reaction by reflecting emotional turmoil back at you.

These emotional patterns can be general, or they can be specific; only we will know.

If it's general, it's just the emotion key, and it's not tied to the experience.

If it's specific, the emotional key is tied to the experience.

For our example, general would be areas of life in which this group felt disgusted with themselves because they had been innocently been taken advantage of. Specific would be tied to the experience; in this case, it's sexual, and so the reflection this group would be looking for would be tied to a sexual experience where disgust and being taken advantage of are present. This specific reflection can be for any experience where sex is the basis of the issue, and that can be through anyone, not just a paedophile, as you will see in the specific examples.

If we don't address our emotions in our lives because we are not aware of them and have pushed them to the background, the will appear in the emotional patterns that keep repeating in life. Even if these patterns are being denied within, they cannot be denied on the outside. Someone or something completely random will reflect this back to you and cause you to have an emotional reaction. That's why something completely unrelated to your own experience can trigger your stuff. It's not really them you are reacting to—it's an inner part of you that needs healing and clearing.

The best way to explain this is through examples of both general and specific reflections, all of which clients have presented with over the years. Let's continue to use our paedophile example as the cause of the emotion reaction. Can you find the key points of disgust, being taken advantage of, and innocence in my examples?

General Examples

Someone has the lesson of attention with the lesson of abandonment. A woman has put all her time and effort in keeping her partner happy and looking after the children and family home. She has neglected her own needs (abandoning herself) in the process and has put on a lot of weight. Her ungrateful partner is constantly making rude and hurtful remarks about her weight.

The emotional reflection is that she feels taken for granted (taken advantage of) by her ungrateful husband, and she's disgusted with herself for putting so much effort into him that she neglected herself. The more she puts up with this situation, and the more disgusted she feels for allowing herself to taken for granted, the more this will be internally triggered and reflected back to her by someone like this paedophile.

Someone else has the lesson of security with the lesson of achievement. A man put his trust and savings in the hands of another person, and he got ripped off and lost it all. Now he has to work harder to try to secure his family's future.

The emotional reflection is that he is feeling disgusted with himself for making such a bad decision that resulted in him getting ripped off and losing the family's security. The more anger he holds on to because of this situation, the more his anger is going to be internally triggered and reflected back to him by someone like this paedophile.

Someone has the lesson of stability with the lesson of support. This girl has been overly supporting others at work to her own detriment, and her work fell behind. When she needed help, no one stepped up to give her the help she gave them.

The emotional reflection she is feeling is disgust with herself for allowing others to take advantage of her kind nature. The more she holds onto the resentment of being let down and taken advantage of, the more this will be internally triggered and reflected back to her by someone like this paedophile.

Specific Examples

Someone has the lesson of independence with the lesson of abandonment. This person was sexually abused and has been left feeling violated and disgusted, and now she is self-abusing with a negative self-view, guilt, shame, and alcohol.

The more these inner feelings of abuse and self-abuse are left unaddressed, the more these feelings are going to be internally triggered and reflected back to her by someone like the paedophile.

Someone has the lesson of self-worth with the lesson of acceptance. This sensitive girl was taken advantage of by a male who said he loved her, and then as soon as they had sex, he rejected her. She was left feeling disgusted with her own sexuality because she thought her performance mustn't have been good enough for him to reject her so badly.

The more she hangs on to these beliefs about her sexual worthiness and rejection, the more these feelings will be internally triggered and reflected back by someone like the paedophile.

Someone has the lesson of control with the lesson of freedom. This gay male fell hard for a partner who withheld sex to manipulate him and get him to do what he wanted. This male did things he didn't want to do for fear he would lose the love of his life, which left him feeling violated and manipulated.

The longer he holds onto this relationship or the feelings of being violated and manipulated, the more this is likely to be internally triggered and reflected back to him by someone like a paedophile.

Of course, the "someone like the paedophile" in our examples means it is someone who triggers the key emotional points of disgust, being let down, and innocence. It doesn't have to actually be a paedophile, just someone who triggers these emotions through his or her behaviour.

All these examples are general and only use one soul lesson. The majority of you will have more than one soul lesson, creating a filter of its own. It may be a single soul lesson reflection or a number of them; maybe it's all of them in combination. You will need to dig deep. When you find the reflection in your own emotions and in your own life, you can then work towards healing it and changing it.

Wisdom Note: Other people's bad behaviour is never a reflection of you—it's a reflection of them and the depth they have shut out and blocked their own hearts and feelings. This doesn't mean you don't deal with issues or problems that others present to you. Bad behaviour is still bad behaviour, and we shouldn't put up with it. You will still have to deal with it. Doing this work will show you whether you are meant to confront another person, stand up for yourself and your rights, or chalk it up as a learning experience.

At this stage, we are digging out the soul lesson reflections through our judgements and looking for them in our own emotional reflections. In the shift sanctuary and the workshops I hold, participants are not always able to see them at first, but they are always there. You cannot see it in another if it is not within you.

Here are a few more simple reflections with a couple of prompters to help you determine what your individual reflection really is. Knowing your own soul lessons is going to help.

Judgement: Someone keeps lying to you.

Reflection: Where are you not being honest with yourself or others?

+ Where in your life do you bend the truth and tell little white lies?
+ Do you justify and lie to yourself?

Judgement: Someone let you down and didn't give you the support you wanted.

Reflection: Where are you letting yourself or others down with a lack of support?

+ Do you say no to support, or support others in detriment to yourself?
+ Are you supporting yourself in your own life with health, well-being, finances, or work direction?

Judgement: Everyone keeps taking, and no one is ever there for you when you need them.

Reflection: Where is your own giving and receiving out of balance with yourself or others?

- Do you give in detriment to self?
- Do you know how to receive?
- Are you too busy giving to others that you are neglecting yourself?

Judgement: You are sick of people breaking their commitments.

Reflection: Where do you break your own commitments to yourself and others?

- Do your break your own commitments in order to keep others happy?
- Do you start things but never finish them?

Judgement: Someone is controlling you, and you're sick of being told what to do.

Reflection: Where in your life are you being controlling?

- Are you good at controlling your emotions so that no one else can see your pain?
- Are you overly pedantic in the home with cleaning, or at work with standards that are too high?
- Are you obsessive about your appearance or weight?

Now you should be able to see your reflection in the mirror of your own judgement. The next step is to look at the reflection and see whether it is real, imagined, and self-created. This will also help you determine your next step in regards to how you move forward.

Step 4: What's Imagined, Real, and Created?

In this step, we are going to further break down our perception of a situation. We now want to look at how much this emotional reaction has affected your own perceptions. Are they real? Are they imagined? How much of your own behaviour through these perceptions is directly affecting and creating your outcomes? Remember that the ego can create the very thing it fears most.

In other words, how much is your emotional filter affecting the way you are perceiving a situation to be, and thus creating it? What's real, what's imagined, and what's created? You have to know what you need to change in order to change it. It could be a program, or it could be your own behaviour; perhaps it's both. This step will help you uncover the part you are playing in your own pain.

We can perceive something that is a presumption or opinion that isn't factual. By looking deeper into our own judgements and the judgements of others, we can determine whether these perceptions are real. We may need to change our perceptions based on these facts, or we may find clarity that other people's judgement of us isn't correct and is probably based on their own stuff. This helps us identify what is ours, what is theirs, and what needs changing.

Look at the judgements and soul lessons, and reflect them on to your own behaviour. "Where is this in me? What part of this situation is real or imagined, and what part am I playing in creating it?" Look at the situation and the judgements of all parties to determine the facts. Review your own behaviour and whether it is having an effect on others, which results in you co-creating the experience and your fears. Are any judgements, either theirs or yours, a reflection of an internal view you hold about yourself that you may not have noticed? What programming and internal beliefs are showing up for you to work on and change? View all of this through your experience like an observer on the outside looking in.

The story, your lessons, and the judgement will tell you. I have a form you can download to help you with this process. First, I am going to share with you some case studies of some of my real clients (the names are changed to protect their identities) to further help you understand how this process works.

Case Study 1: Sandra

Issue/Judgement

Sandra told me she had an overwhelming fear of networking, so much so that she would approach a networking event, sit in the car, and work herself up by telling herself that everyone will think she is crazy (she is an energy healer). Her anxiety would become so intense that she wouldn't go in and would drive home.

The Soul Lessons

Sandra's lessons are 34/7.

> 3. Self-worth, the lesson of acceptance
> 4. Stability, the lesson of support
> 7. Trust, the lesson of belief

Define the Key Emotions with the Soul Lessons

First, we look at her story, judgement, and perception of the situation. We define it with Sandra's soul lessons. She was perceiving and believing (7) that she wouldn't get support (4) and acceptance (3) from the group. She didn't feel confident enough (3) to go in.

Real or Imagined

Were her thoughts real or imagined? She was perceiving what may happen. It may not have happened, so her fear was an imagined, perceived thought. It felt real to her at the time, but because she didn't go in, it never happened and therefore was imagined.

Reflection

In her reflection of her soul lessons and key emotional points, she identified that she needed to work on her own inner programming and learn to believe in herself (7) and accept herself as being worthy of other people's acceptance

(3) and support (4). We took this deeper by reflecting where this behaviour was showing up in her own life, and we found that Sandra was very good at supporting others (4) but didn't believe (7) she was worthy (3) of support (4) from others. She often rejected help because she didn't want to be a burden; even with little gestures of offered assistance, she would reject them by saying, "No, I am okay, thanks." Not only was she believing she would be rejected and unsupported by the group, but she herself was rejecting others when they tried to offer support to her. Sandra was doing to herself what she feared most and was trying to protect herself from.

Sandra's aha moment helped her see where she needed to step up in own confidence and beliefs, and also where she needed to address her own behaviour by learning to accept support—something she wasn't even aware of doing.

As an exercise, let's go a bit further and imagine what could have happened if Sandra had gone into the meeting with her fears and emotional reaction, just to help you understand how we can create what we fear.

Creating

Remember that she is sensitive to people not accepting or believing in her, and she felt anxious and nervous. Think of the energy she would then present to the people she would meet. Do you think her anxiety and nervousness would be present in her presentation and dealings with others? How would other people perceive this? How would you perceive an anxious, nervous person trying to sell you something? Could she be perceived as being incompetent or not knowing her stuff though her nervousness? Could people then feel she wasn't right for them to work with and reject her? Could this then create the circumstance she feared the most? If she had gone into the meeting when she felt so emotionally unstable, then I believe she very well could have created her own fears, which would have knocked her confidence even more.

Case Study 2: Kayla

Issue/Judgement

Kayla had a partner who was judging her on the amount of money she was earning through her business. Her partner actually told her that she needed to get a "real" job. (She worked for herself as intuitive coach and healer. In his perception, a real job was working for someone else.)

Kayla's judgement of him and his suggestion that she needed to get a real job was that he was a controlling jerk who thought that nothing she did financially was good enough. She was very angry with her partner for trying to stop her from following her dreams.

The Soul Lessons

Her soul lessons are 35/8.

> 3. Self-worth, the lesson of acceptance
> 5. Control, the lesson of freedom
> 8. Security, the lesson of achievement

Define the Key Emotions with the Soul Lessons

Her hissy fit and judgement of him, and his suggestion that she needed to get a real job, meant that he was controlling (5) and that nothing she ever did financially (8) was ever good enough (3).

Real or Imagined

When we reflected this back to Kayla, she could ask herself whether his judgement of her was real or imagined.

First, she looked at the facts. How much did she earn, how much does a "real job" pay, what did she contribute financially to the relationship, and was it balanced? She discovered there was no way she could afford to get a real job. A real job at the average wage would barely cover her business expenses, let alone what she was contributing in the home, the travel she loved to do, and the contribution she was making to others through creating her trainings and products. She was making far more than the average wage.

Reflection

Her partner's judgement of her, in her opinion, was an imagined judgement and not real, however it pushed her buttons, it caused a deep emotional reaction within Kayla. That meant she had to own her part in it as well. By looking at her hissy fit and her own judgement of him, which was that he was controlling (5) and that nothing she ever did financially (8) was good enough (3), and then reflecting this back onto herself, she could see through her own beliefs that she didn't think she was good enough (3) to take control (5) of her own financial future and achieve (8) her dreams in her own right without the security of the relationship and the shared financial contribution.

Creating

Although the facts showed she didn't need to get a real job, she did need to work on her confidence and belief in herself so that she could achieve her own financial stability. She identified that her own lack of belief in herself and her ability had her playing small to keep the peace. Having this understanding allowed Kayla to face her own reality and have the courage to make those changes in her own beliefs, which led her to step out of the relationship, and take control of her own financial future, and prove to the only person who really mattered (herself) that she could do it.

Wisdom Note: Ending a relationship should be the last resort, when you have done tones of work to determine how much you are both in reaction and co-contributing to the problems. If it's just your soul lesson reactions pushing you apart, you can often work on these and possibly save the relationship. If you don't do the inner work, chances are you will repeat the same pattern in the next relationship. If you have grown apart because you have evolved into two very different people who now want to head in different directions, then you can agree to set each other free and move forward. Kayla's decision was the latter, and it wasn't taken lightly. It was a mutual decision in which these two people ended as friends, and as far as I know, they are still good friends today.

Case Study 3: Ellie

Issue/Judgement

Ellie was having an issue at work. A work colleague was pushing her buttons because she was flirting with all the males in the office. They would then play up to her flirting, and thus they would all fall behind in their work, making Ellie's job harder because she was left to pick up the slack and do their work as well as her own.

Soul Lessons

Ellie's lesson is 13/4. She also has the 2 lesson because of the duality of 1 and 2.

> 1. Independence, the lesson of abandonment
> 2. Codependence, the lesson of attention
> 3. Self-worth, the lesson of acceptance
> 4. Stability, the lesson of support.

Define the Key Emotions with the Soul Lessons

First, we looked at the judgement and defined her soul lesson. She was judging the girl as an attention seeker (2) and her colleagues for abandoning (1) their work and not being supportive (4) of her, which made her feel devalued. (3).

Real or Imagined

Was her judgement real or imagined? It was a real problem because it was affecting her work. People were not doing their jobs, and thus it was affecting her ability to do her job, which put extra pressure on her. Other people's behaviour would need to be addressed for this situation to change.

Reflection

Then we reflected this back onto her. Where was she doing this behaviour, and what emotional buttons were being pushed? She discovered that she was abandoning herself (1) by not standing up for herself and asking for the help and support she needed (4), because she feared they wouldn't like her (3) or she would be rejected, picked on, or bullied by the others for having a say and confronting them (1).

Creating

She determined that the behaviour that needed to change in the office was also hers. She needed to step up by addressing the issue with others, because she was co-creating this situation by not standing up and asking for the help and support she needed. She identified that both her beliefs and her behaviour needed to be worked on and changed.

Case Study 4: Emily

Issue/Judgement

Emily was upset with her mother. She had planned an overseas trip, and her mother suggested a more expensive option because her mum thought she would see more and it would be more comfortable for Emily. Her mother told her that she would lend her the extra money, but when the time came, due to unforeseen circumstances, her mother didn't have the funds to lend her. Emily had to borrow the money from the bank, which was more expensive, and now she had a bigger debt to pay. She felt her mother had lied to her and that if she had gone with her original plans, she wouldn't be in so much debt.

Soul Lessons

Emily's soul lessons are 26/8. She also has the 1 lesson because of the duality of 1 and 2.

2. Codependence, the lesson of attention

1. Independence, the lesson of abandonment

6, Commitment, the lesson of sharing

8. Security, the lesson of achievement

Define the Key Emotions with the Soul Lessons

Ellie felt her mother had lied to her and let her down (1) by not doing what she said she was going to do (6). She blamed her mother for the debt she was now in (8).

Real or Imagined

The problem is real Emily now owes the money to the bank because her mother couldn't help her pay.

Reflection

While Emily was telling me about her anger towards her mother, she also told me that she was already suffering from an unexpected debt because she had incorrectly reported her wage to Centrelink for her study allowance, and they had over paid her. She now had to pay that money back to Centrelink as well as her holiday. I helped her see that the anger she had at her mother was for the exact same behaviour she had done herself. Because of her incorrect reporting to Centrelink (1), money she was entrusted and obligated to pay (6) was not paid and ended up as a debt that was unwanted (8). In truth, she was really angry at her own behaviour rather than her mother's, and by seeing she had also done the exact same behaviour she was accusing her mother of, it helped Emily take more responsibility for her reaction and calmed down the situation.

Creating

Emily could see that she was creating more debt for herself every time she abandoned her own commitments and values when it came to money and finances. I am really proud of Emily, she is young, and if she can start to own and be responsible for her emotional reactions at this young age, she will be way ahead in the future. Good on you, Emily.

These case studies should help you understand how to reflect and dig out your own emotional reactions and any part you play in creating situations. Remember that it has shown up in your life, it's pushing your buttons, and it's emotionally affecting you because it's a reflection of you and what you are meant to be learning. Every situation will be different, and as previously mentioned, you will sometimes have all lessons showing up, or you may only have one or two.

When we don't see the part we play, we keep repeating the behaviour and attracting and creating the same emotional pattern. It may show up in a different situation, but the emotional reaction will be the same.

Here are the key parts to identifying a soul lesson reaction.

1. Have your hissy fit with purpose, and write out your story with your perceptions and judgements.
2. Find your emotional balance, which will allow you to consciously connect to the situation.
3. Do the self-reflection. Where is your soul lesson judgement showing up within you?
4. Is it real or imagined, and how much are you responsible for creating or co-creating it? Do you need to change your inner beliefs, or do you also need to change your behaviour and address other people's behaviours?

As mentioned previously, I have a step-by-step system called "Unpacking Your Soul Lessons." You can download it to help you go through the process. You can find this on my website at www.juliekayinternational. com/freestuff.

This may take a bit of practise, but once it clicks in, you will become an old pro in no time, and you will be digging out the real issues for both yourself and others, gaining a deeper understanding to what is really going on in every interaction.

Now the magic can begin because you finally know what you didn't know— what life has been trying to tell you all along. You can make changes and break out of the emotional patterns keeping you stuck. Hallelujah!

Let's take a moment and review.

This is pretty deep stuff, right? My suggestion to people who are first learning to go within and self-reflect is to learn to understand how to dig out the ego reaction. Your ego is very good at hiding this stuff and burying it deep inside; it's had plenty of practise because it's been doing it for years. Give yourself time to expose it. I have been doing this work for many years, so if you get stuck and need help, I can expose your lessons and their stuff in no time at all. If needed, book a session with me; I have a special offer at the end of the book.

There are two main points to reflect on when digging out the ego reactions.

1. Where is both the judgement of others and your own judgement showing up in the reflection of your own beliefs and actions?
2. Do these beliefs and actions play any part in you creating or co-creating the situation that is pushing your buttons?

This will show you the hidden beliefs and behaviours of your ego—and exactly what it is you need to heal and change to move forward.

Every time you have an emotional reaction, you will learn to expose it for what it is and what you are meant to be learning. Remember that it is often the same emotional pattern showing up in different circumstances.

Believe me, this is the hardest part of the whole book, but it's the part that is going to change your life and get you unstuck. Take your time and have a break if you need, but keep going. Read steps 3 and 4 over and over again until you get it. When you feel you understand how it works, you're ready to make some changes and start to heal. That's in the next section, so when you're ready, I will see you there.

CHAPTER 7

The Consciously Connected Mind, Body, and Soul

> Overcome your barriers, intend the best, and be patient.
> You will enjoy more balance, more growth, more income,
> and more fun!
>
> —Jack Canfield

Are you ready to make the changes and move forward? Great! Now, if you were sitting in front of me, we could work out a more personalised approach to your direction forward, because everyone is different and learns in different ways. Some people only need a bit of help, whereas others need a lot. The best way to address this in a book is to give you some of the best of what I know. You can guide yourself in what you feel you need to move forward. There is so much out there that can help you in your healing, but as you are reading this book, I am going to guide you with what has worked for both me and my clients.

From here on in, I am also going to be prompting you to start making conscious contact with your own spirit and let it be your guide. Your internal self knows what healing and changes are needed, and your subconscious will try to reveal this to you. What you need will resonate with you, will jump out at you, and will feel right for you. It may have already been popping into your mind, niggling at you. The spirit is very good at showing us what we need through these very simple ways, and then the ego jumps in and confuses us or convinces us to stay in our comfort zones because it's easier.

Easier is not where we find the spirit's inspiration and purpose. I am much more comfortable sloshing around the house in my twenty-year-old UGG boots and Sloppy Joe than I am all dressed up for a business meeting, but sloshing around the house won't get me what I want. If we were able to fulfil our destinies in our comfort zones, then there would be a lot more people living their purpose and dreams.

Will healing stop the issues in your life? No. You're living in the physical world, and we are never going to stop evolving and learning. We learn a lot though our issues. What healing will give you, however, is the inner strength to get through the issues quickly, with balance, and with a lot less emotional turmoil. We really are like onions: peel off one layer, and there is another underneath. However, the emotional turmoil gets less and less, and you get more peace and happiness. Life will just keep getting better, but you will always have issues, and life will always present challenges that are out of our control. This is life, and even Jesus, Mahatma Gandhi, and Mother Theresa had issues and challenges to face.

The less overthinking and emotional turmoil you have, the more you are allowing your spirit the space to guide you. You will become more intuitive because the mind and its overthinking is the main thing blocking your intuition. Any ego beliefs and perception that you hold about your intuitive ability and whether you have it or not will block you as well. You can do it, you were born with intuition, and you were consciously connected before you formed your ego. Your ego came later, and whether it's reconnecting now while you're still in your physical body, or later when you return to spirit, you will be consciously connected again. The when is up to you through your own conscious choice; it's a decision you will make to start listening to your spirit rather than the ranting of your ego.

Let's start our healing with the three systems of self. These three systems of self are linked and form a vital part in keeping you balanced. You have heard the old cliché "Mind, body, and soul." This phrase has stood the test of time because it truly defines the connection these three parts of us have to each other and the ability of one part to affect the other. I first spoke about this in my very first book, *The Missing Link*, back in 2007. I refer to the mind, body, and soul connection as the three systems of self. If you have one system out of balance, it will have an effect on the others and drag them out of balance. Therefore I feel it's vital in the healing process to address all three.

Here is a basic example for each.

If your mind is out of balance, this will affect your physical body through stress. Most people understand this, so I won't need to go into much detail. If you don't, simply google the effects of stress on the human body, and you will see what I am talking about,

If your body is out of balance, with poor diet and no exercise, your brain is not getting the right nutrients. It's not healthy, and you have a dull mind and low energy. Low energy equals a low emotional state, which brings on depression, bringing your mind out of balance.

If you soul is out of balance, you are not consciously connected to your inner well-being, peace, and happiness. This gives more power to the intellectual ego side of self and your worries, which bring your mind out of balance.

If we are out of balance in one system of self, it has a direct effect on the others.

For healing, I am going to break up this chapter into three sections and give you guidance for all three. There are many ways to heal, and so I will give you some of the best that I have found for each.

Go with what feels right for you; that will be your spirit talking. If your mind says, "I'm not doing that"—in other words, there is an emotional reaction to something—then do it just to teach your ego a lesson, because the emotional reaction will be your ego talking.

The Mind

Your mind has created the belief and perceptions that you have identified in the last section. It is both a mental and emotional program that you have formed as your belief. The depth of this belief has been ingrained by repetition. Every time you had a thought or an emotional reaction, your perceptional belief was ingrained a little more.

What do you think would happen if we told a child right from birth that it was good for nothing? Do you think that child would take on that belief and become good for nothing? Our jails are filled with good-for-nothing people who have been born into, and then bought into, that program and belief.

This is your soul lesson programming, and although it may not be as bad as my example, you are telling yourself something that you have been believing: a pattern of thought that keeps you believing that you are or you aren't something.

The repetition of this makes the belief stronger. I feel that if repetition can put it there, then repetition can form a new belief.

The brain is wired for habit. Habitual thinking is the result of the nervous system firing specific neurons in order. An impulse originates in the cell body of a neuron and travels to the end of the neuron, which is then communicated to the next neuron across a synaptic gap. With each connection via the communicated impulse, the neurons become more closely associated, creating a neural pathway in the brain. Repetitious thoughts fire the same neurons in the same order and sequence, which over time results in habitual thoughts and behaviours that can be hard to change.

We know we can't remove an old, ingrained neural pathway, but we can create a new one through neuroplasticity. I also learnt that the old pathways, because of their strength, will be what we revert back to; they will be our comfort zones until the new pathway is strong enough to take over.

Professor of Neuroscience Anne Graybiel found in her studies that new neuron patterns can be formed with a new habit, only to revert back to the old neuron pattern again if something kicks off the old habit. This is why it is difficult to change a habit: your brain and its neural pathways are working against you.

I like to explain it like this: Let's imagine that for years, you have walked along the same path through the bush, day in and day out, hail or shine. Over those years, the pathway you have walked has become deep and clear. It wasn't always like that when you first started; it was overgrown and hard to see. In time, with you repetitiously walking the path, it became clearer and easier for you, and you no longer had to watch your every step. You simply walked the path on autopilot.

One day, you decide to make a new path because it was going to be quicker. This path, however, has rocks and grass and twigs on it, so it's not as clear, comfortable or as easy as the other path to navigate; you have to be very conscious of where you are walking. Then a few days later, while walking along, you trip over a rock and say, "Shove it. This is too hard. It's easier to go back to the old path." You go back to it because it's clearer and easier, even though it's not the way you really want to go.

This is you and your habits, and the pathways are your neural pathways. Over time, they are deeply ingrained and habitual. We can create new ones and new habits, but only conscious effort, repetition, and time will make them easy and clear. If you had persevered over time, the new pathway through the bush would have become deeper and clearer, just like the old one. If something kicks off an old habit, we will return to it and the old neural pathways. How many times have you given up on doing something because it was hard? How many times have you given up on trying to change a habit and are frustrated because you haven't been successful? Not anymore, I hope. I hope you understand that the new neural pathway you have been trying to create simply wasn't strong enough yet. Now, I hope you can jump straight back to the new one without frustration, because now you know why.

To create a new neural pathway, we can repeat, repeat, and repeat a new thought or behaviour to ingrain it and make it stronger than the last, as well as identify any triggers that will have you reverting back to the same behaviour. Self-awareness will help you see any emotional patterns and behaviours that set you off, and your emotional soul lesson triggers are a good place to start.

When you want to change something, you will have to change the belief system, and the belief was created via perception and thought. Thoughts are created in the intellectual mind. Change your thoughts, and you change your life! How many times have you heard this? It's not as easy as that, though, is it? You will have to change the neural pathways and belief systems as well. If you want to change a habit, start with a new thought and behaviour and repeat, repeat, repeat to create a new neural pathway.

Here are my tips for changing the belief patterns and neural pathways.

"I Am" Statements

Whatever you believe, you achieve. If you don't believe you can do something you won't be able to do it. What you believe about yourself is what you will see. If you believe you are fat, then you see yourself as fat even if those around you tell you otherwise. Anorexia is a perfect example.

The first thing to change is the belief. You haven't always had that belief; it was formed through your programming and experiences, through the ego side of self. As an example I used previously in regards to a child being programmed into the belief of being good for nothing, you can change your belief in the same way: by repetition, even if your ego does not believe it to start with.

You won't believe a new program to start with because you are still believing the old one. Over time, the new one will settle into your neural pathways, and your mind, body, and soul will start to respond to the new belief system and neural pathways.

It can be hard to tell yourself, "I am healthy and thin," when all you see in the mirror is that you are overweight. Every time you look in the mirror and say, "God, I am fat," think about how depressed you feel. That depressed feeling calls out to you from the refrigerator, and if you're not strong enough, you will give in to it—and the cycle repeats. If you decide to change the program with, "I am thinner and healthy," and repeat it over and over, then after a while, you will feel your inner strength grow, and you will start to think and feel more empowered, which stops you giving in to the callings of the refrigerator. Then you lose a little bit of weight, you start to believe you can do it, and presto—twelve months down the track, you are not only healthy and hot, but you also believe you are.

I like to use the "I am" statements. I heard one of my favourite teachers, Wayne Dyer, talk about the power of the "I am" statement many years ago. He stated "I am" as being the word of God, the creative power behind who we are and become. What you state yourself to be, you will be, what you tell yourself you are, you will become it because you are already doing this through your "I am" statements. Your "I am" statement is your belief. "I am fat, I am broke, I am not good enough, I am useless at this, I am stressed, I am depressed." If you have used any of these statements recently, then you are cementing them as your reality, and you will continue to create more of the same. It's time to start creating a new reality, and you can do that through new "I am" statements.

Whatever you are trying to change through your soul lessons, make it an "I am" statement. You may wish to work on something specific, or you may want to work on your soul lessons as a combination. I say both. Specifically, you can work on something that you believe about yourself that you know you need to change in order to move forward.

> If you have a self-worth lesson: "I am worthy of ..." (add what your worthy of)
> If you have a support lesson: "I am supported in ..." (and add what your supported in)

I have created an "I am" statement for all the soul lesson combinations in chapter 5. Feel free to use this for your specific soul lesson combination, or make up your own.

If you have a belief that you're overweight: "I am healthy and looking good."

If you are always saying, "I am broke," change it to, "I am abundant, and money comes to me effortlessly and easily."

You will have to nag yourself to death with it and use it often. You can't just say it a couple of times a day and expect it to form a new belief and habitual way of thinking. You will need to nag yourself over and over again. I suggest you do this when you're driving, when you're walking, when you are doing mundane jobs like cleaning, or when you're going to the toilet. Your mind will be thinking about something, so you may as well direct it into thinking about something that will help you rather than hinder you. When your old beliefs pop in, redirect them by replacing them with your "I am" mantra.

If you really want to get your "I am" belief ingrained into a neural pathway quicker, then do the above, and once a day, get a piece of paper and write your "I am" mantra out over and over until it fills the paper. Start today; this is something you can do anywhere.

When changing a habit or creating a new belief, it is very easy to go back to the old one when life gets in the way, so it's a great idea to have something that can trigger you to remember that you are changing this old habit—something that makes you stop, balance, and get back on track with the new habit.

Here are some examples that can help you to remember.

- Screen savers on your mobile or computer that align with your new "I am."
- Set an alarm on your phone with your "I am" statement twice a day
- Gratitude journal or daily journal. Ask yourself, "How did I do today?"
- Place your "I am" affirmations around the house.
- Participate in a support group.
- Create a support network of like-minded friends.
- Buy a significant piece of jewellery to remind you. (I wear a cross to remind me I am guided.)
- Some of the Shift Sisters, ladies who have done the Shift Sanctuary training decided they wanted a constant reminder to balance. I had a tattoo designed of a lotus and yin/yang symbol for those who wanted to use it as a visual reminder to balance and keep connected to their spirits.

+ Put love, hope, and faith wooden signs around your house; this helps reflect this energy to others too.

+ Remember that everything that you state you are, you will be because you have created it as a belief. Change the belief, and you will change who you are.

Creative Visualisation: A Class in Intuition

Visualisation is a form of imagination, using your mind to see what you want to see and attracting it to you. I am going to give you a short class in intuition. If you look back to the beginning of the book to my picture of the torus, you will see in the energy pattern of the torus that there is a funnel-like flow of energy entering at the top of the head. We call this the crown chakra. This funnel of energy flow creates what we call a channel. It is the entry point for all that we can consciously channel through the subconscious from beyond.

We can channel healing energy, the intuitive, and the creative through this channel, drawing on these energies and bringing them into our reality and the physical realm.

Channelling the intuition is intentionally connecting to the subconscious for direction and to gain guidance and messages from your higher self, guides, and even loved ones who have passed.

Channelling healing energy is bringing in a high vibrational form of energy for the purpose of healing. You may have heard of DLF therapy or Reiki.

Channelling the creative is when we draw on inspiration and ideas to enhance our lives through any form of creativity.

There is a special key to opening this channel. Wait for it, because this is huge ... It's called imagination. Yes, that part of you that you keep thinking, "Was that just my imagination?" Consider this. Everything that has ever been created here on the earth plane has had to come from someone's imagination. It didn't exist until people created the thought, and they then created it. If you have ever experienced a healing session like DLF therapy or Reiki, then the therapist is using imagination to imagine the healing light coming in to heal. Healers even use their imaginations to heal people who are not present through absentee healing. When I am talking to loved ones who have passed, I imagine that spirit is stepping forward, and it does. The imagination is not what is coming through the channel; the imagination is what opens the channel for whatever you're imagining to then flow through.

If you imagine that you are creating something, the imagination opens the channel, and the thought you need to create it comes through.

If you imagine that you are healing someone, the imagination opens the channel, and the healing light comes through.

If you imagine you are intuitive, your imagination opens the channel, and the intuitive flows through. When you use your imagination, you are making direct, conscious contact with your spirit. You send the intellectual mind to the background during this time as your creative, subconscious mind takes over.

Usually it's the other way around: the subconscious is relegated to the background. But when you use your imagination, you are sending the intellect to the background. This is where you can take control of creating the life you wish.

In my classes where I have taught people to tap into spirits or their intuitions, I ask them to use their imaginations and see what happens. They never cease to blow themselves away with the accuracy of their so-called imaginations.

It puts a bit of different spin on, "Was that just my imagination?" The part that opened the channel for whatever it was you saw or experienced was indeed imagination.

If you can imagine it, you can create it and receive it. If you want to create a wonderful relationship or happier life, start imagining it. If there are blocks to this via your soul lessons, you will attract what you need to unblock this first, but you will still be moving towards it.

As an example, you are trying to attract a relationship, but your soul lessons are reflecting a worthiness issue. You will attract the soul lesson reflection to clear this either before or through your new relationship.

You can combine the "I am" mantra with your visualisation. Whatever you are stating, you can also visualise and see it as being so, and therefore it helps change your neural pathways even faster.

Wisdom Note: When I was in grade two, my parents took me along to a teacher-parent interview. The teacher was highly disappointed that I couldn't focus and was often in my own little world, and she found this frustrating. She told my parents not to expect much from me academically. What the …? I was in grade two, for god's sake. Clearly at that age, I was more creative and connected to my spirit, just like a lot of the sensitive souls entering the world now. I left school in year eleven, and since then I have achieved a lot academically via further study. My life's purpose, however, is more creative and intuitive, which was not learnt at school.

I feel we can really do damage by inflicting our values and views onto others and trying to make society fit in one big comfortable box. Being told that you are not good enough forms the programming that we carry with us. Be careful what you say to others—your words can cause issues for many years to come. We are all unique and have come here to experience our uniqueness. Nobody should tell you who you are, tell you what you should believe, or judge your beliefs. This is the basis of disconnection in the world. If we could accept each other and our different beliefs, the world would be a much better place. We still have a way to go yet, but let's start with me and you.

I believe it's time the education system also acknowledges that not all children learn academically. It's time that we bring in more creative, hands-on ways of teaching to our schools for the children who are creative and active and who learn better through doing rather than the traditional textbook way. Creative kids get bored, and when children are bored, they are going to act out.

If your child struggles at school with her learning, she is probably more creative, and her talents will be in something that aligns to being creative. Look up her soul gifts when you get to that section. Not everyone is meant to be a scholar, and just because you are not gifted in academics, that doesn't mean you will achieve less. Richard Branson, founder of the Virgin Group is dyslexic. Steve Jobs, the founder of Apple, and Michael Dell, the founder of Dell Technologies, never completed college.

Just because you or your kids don't fit into the system or have been labelled by teachers or others as not smart enough, you have a purpose and something you are good at, something at which you can excel. You simply need to discover what that is.

Flip it—And Flip It Good!

We have learnt that there is a yin and a yang side to everything. If there is a problem, there must be a solution. If there is challenge, there must a gift. If there is a lesson, then there must be a learning. If one side is out of balance, go and find the other; flip it.

If your ego is feeling unsupported by someone, flip it and find where else the support is coming from. Focus on this. It may not be coming from the one you want it to come from, but it will be there—you just need to start noticing it.

The more you notice and focus on something, the more it will show up. If you focus and notice only lack, you are sending out for more. Flip it! Be grateful and focus on what you do have.

The ego loves to focus on the problem, and this can go around and around in your mind, thinking of the injustice of it all. Flip it to find the solution.

You may have experienced something that was out of your control and left you feeling injured. Flip it and find the blessing.

Let me flip my experience of sexual abuse. This experience could very well have saved my life a few years later. As you would expect, this experience left me a little untrusting and wary of men. A few years later, an extended family member and I were visiting an area in which my immediate family used to live. We were walking down the road when a man tried to pull me into his car. I got away, ran up the street, and got help from a lady who was driving a baker's delivery van, delivering bread in the neighbourhood. The family member with me thought the man was mucking around and tried to tell the lady we were okay. I was terrified and hysterical, and no way was I letting this lady drive off without me. She let us get into the van, and as we drove past the man in the car, he jumped into the road, waving and pointing at me as he tried to stop her. She dropped us off to my very grateful parents. They were furious, and it still haunts this family member who was with me today; she told me so at a family get-together earlier this year.

Had I not had that untrusting wariness of men from my first experience, I may have let her talk me out of this being a dangerous situation. I may not have gotten away from the man the second time around.

My experience of abuse has also helped me help others. I understand what it is like to carry the emotional baggage of that experience and the effects it can have for many years to come, until we heal it.

By flipping it and finding my blessings, I am so grateful that I was not pulled into that man's car that day, and I can now help others with genuine compassion and understanding.

The miracle is always in front; the teaching is behind. Don't let your past set the path for your future. Find your blessing and your miracles.

Meditation

I have mentioned before that meditation is a practise to help you bring your thoughts into balance. Mindful meditation or a guided meditation is a great way to start. You can choose a meditation for whatever it is you want to achieve in your life: balance, sleep, calmness. You can even find a meditation to attract love into your life. I have a free meditation called "Calling in Love." Use this for attracting whatever you would love to have in your life right now. To listen to it, go to https://www.youtube.com/watch?v=K7IFdXSOi4A.

Who Are You Feeding, Your Spirit or Your Ego?

Feed the ego, and you fall behind—feed the spirit, and you will shine.

"If you give the ego what it wants, you will not get what you want." Full stop! That's the message I have come up with and have pasted on my own mirror. When I am feeling lazy and uninspired, I ask myself who I'm feeding. It snaps me out of it quickly because I have too much I want to do, attract, and achieve, and I don't want to waste time going back into the ego's old patterns. I have got to the tipping point where I simply have to remind myself that in order to achieve my goals, I need to feed my spirit, not my ego.

You feed your ego when you allow your thoughts to dwell in the negative. You feed your ego when you do the things you know you shouldn't do. You feed the ego when you participate in things that are not in alignment with your direction. Every negative thought, word, or action you do feeds your ego and gives this side of you more strength.

We want to feed the spirit instead. We feed our spirit with gratitude, positive thinking, talking, and action by imagining, visualising, meditating, and connecting to anything creative. Doing things that inspire us, empower us, and help us feel happy from within. Reading this book is feeding your spirit. Eating healthy and exercising is feeding your spirit.

Ask yourself daily, "Who am I feeding today, my ego or my spirit?" Identify any thoughts, behaviours, and actions that are feeding your ego, and change them by replacing them with something that feeds your spirit.

The Body

Of course, feeding your ego can very much relate to actually feeding the ego through eating or drinking what we know isn't good for us but we continue to eat or drink it anyway.

I am a strong believer in a clear and clean diet. However, consciously connected people listen to their own gut instinct and allow their bodies to show them what agrees with them or not.

157

There are so many diets out there, and so many people are becoming sensitive to food that we never used to be sensitive to. Fresh food is generally okay, but it's what is done to the food that is going to make it good or bad for us. I feel we need to be more mindful of the choices we make, and if something isn't agreeing with us, we shouldn't eat it. Learn to tune into your stomach and how what you're eating and drinking is making you feel. If you stay consciously connected to your spirit, it will nag you with the changes you need to make; Guides and loved ones who have passed also like to join in with the nagging if you are not listening.

Ask anyone who had a soft drink addiction, which is full of sugar, how much clearer his mind is since he gave it up. Sugar and sugary processed foods dull the brain. How do you feel after a night of drinking?

Everything in moderation is fine. I am only prompting you to look at how you are treating your body because how you treat it is going to affect your conscious connection.

My view on alcohol as a psychic medium is that spirits and spirits don't mix. I know firsthand that drinking affects my energy and ability to get a good connection. If I am working, I don't drink the night before; on the very odd occasion I do, I know I will find my work harder the next day, and it's not worth it. I like a glass or two of champagne every now and again. knowing it will have an effect on my energy levels and mind the next day. That's a conscious choice I make because I like to have the odd drink with friends and family.

You really don't need me to bang on about the importance of exercise. You have probably heard or read about it a million times, so you know, right? Exercising is feeding your spirit.

For those people who have overactive minds—and I'm one of them—I have found exercise is the best remedy to getting a good night's sleep. I go through periods where nothing I do can balance my mind, not even meditation. I don't know how many times I have woken up in the middle of the night and written an article. If I don't exercise, I find it's worse. I have a creative mind that never shuts up. I'll have three amazing business ideas going around in my head at once. My mind wants to create, and it drives me nuts at night. If I exercise, it calms down. Try it and see if it works for you.

The Soul

The soul is the authentic, beautiful, innocent you. It isn't who you look like, the job you do, or how much money you have—it's just you as you are. Your spirit knows this, but your ego may have missed the memo. When you understand that all your lessons are teaching you to love yourself just as you are, you are getting it. When the internal part of you is no longer rocked by the external, you have got it. The reason you are here is to learn to love, and that love starts with you.

Your spirit understands what true love is, and that the power of love is unconditional: There is no "I will love you because," "I will love you if," or "I will love you when"—there is only "I love you."

When you love unconditionally, you can love anyone because you understand and see that anyone and everyone is a reflection of you. In their own unconditional spirits, others are helping you to see the real you and evolve you to your higher purpose of love and light. For this alone, you should love them even more.

To me, unconditional love is bringing the power of the super consciousness (God) to the physical earth plane. There is nothing more powerful in the universe than this consciousness of love, which is its purest in its unconditional form. You are part of this, in essence you are made of it, and so you are also pure love within.

You are not meant to hate those who bring you the experiences that are helping you to discover who you really are. When you hate them, you hate a part of yourself. You are meant to learn through the reflections they are showing you, and to evolve to a higher consciousness of love. It's okay to turn away from them, but don't hate them. Learn from them and give them thanks for showing you this aspect of yourself.

Most of us have unconditional love for our children and fur babies. They will push our buttons, and they have probably caused a few grey hairs in our time, but we love them anyway. We love them unconditionally. As parents, we are not meant to love our children only if they are good and do what we want them to do. In relationships, you are not meant to love your partner only if he or she is romantic, makes you happy, or does what you want him or her to do. You love your partner because you love your partner! And you can love him or her more easily when you love yourself.

This doesn't mean you need to put up with bad behaviour or spend time with someone who isn't in alignment with you. You turn away from what isn't in alignment with you, and you stand up for yourself in a loving and supportive way when you need to do so. The more you fight your wars armed with love, the more you will see its true power. When you project the powerful force of love towards someone who is causing you pain on a subconscious level, that person's soul feels it, and it gives him or her an opportunity to remember his or her true purpose and higher love on this subconscious level. Love can calm people down and bring them out of reaction so that they have an opportunity to make better choices. Try it for yourself next time someone is frustrating or annoying you with negative actions. Send them love and healing, and really mean it. You will see exactly what I mean. There is no higher vibrational energy force in the universe than unconditional love, and this energy can and does create miracles. You too can create your own miraculous life by connecting to this power, which is freely available to all.

Making conscious connection to your spirit means you start to drive your life from within, with love. You listen to the advice that pops in, which you will hear more easily when you are more balanced and believe this is possible.

When you connect more to the feeling side of self, you are able to feel your gut instinct. You can train yourself and your children to do this naturally by talking in the language of feelings. Simply swap the word *think* with *feel*. When you do this, you are subconsciously asking your gut instinct instead of your mind. You are asking the intuitive side of you when you say, "Does this feel right for me?" instead of, "Do I think this is right for me?" Use this language with your kids and keep them connected to their spirits.

I want you to learn to follow your own light, your own spirit, because no one knows better than you what you need. As leaders and teachers, we are here to prompt you in your journey. If anyone else says something that doesn't gel or feel right for you, it probably isn't. Always follow your own light.

Let's review.

I hope this chapter prompted you and helped you identify the areas of mind, body, and soul that you are ready to work on in order to help you move forward. You will fall off the path sometimes, and that is completely normal. For a lot of people, the ego is very strong in its programming. What I want you to know is that if you keep bringing it back to the teachings, it will get better and better as you go along. It's like any habit you have ever tried to change; you simply have to stop and refocus again. Each time you do, your new neural pathways, feelings, and behaviours get stronger.

The next chapter is all about consciously connected wisdom. What does it mean to be consciously connected? How does a consciously connected person show up and act? You will see parts of yourself in this chapter, and also parts you may wish to work on and evolve.

If you make it your intention to show up consciously connected, then your intuition will come naturally, and your life will flow with more joy and happiness. Yes, I feel you're ready to really consciously connect, so start practising today.

CHAPTER 8

Consciously Connected Wisdom

Remember your perception of the world is a reflection of
your state of consciousness.
—Eckhart Tolle

Consciously connected people do certain things that keep them connected;
they think in a certain way and behave in a certain way. I have met a lot
of consciously connected people in my line of work, and I read a lot of
teachings from some well-known consciously connected leaders. You don't
have to be a master teacher to be consciously connected. You can be a loving
mother bringing up her kids, or the person who drives the garbage truck.
It's not a position in life; it's a way of being. In my observation of consciously
connected people, I have noticed that we all have a similar way of showing
up and practising life. I would like to share this with you.

Allow this wisdom to prompt you in your evolvement. Take note of what
resonates with you for any change you wish to make. Chances are your spirit
has been nagging you too, anyway.

Make Yourself Matter

Consciously connected people know the importance of making themselves
matter. One of the reasons we lose ourselves is that we start to unconsciously
put others and everything else before ourselves. You will never find happiness
by always putting yourself on the back burner for others, or because life gets
in the way. Life is always going to get in the way, and you will always be

fighting a losing battle. If you're waiting for the right time to make yourself a priority in your own life, then you have already been waiting too long. Don't waste any more time and start today. Making yourself a priority takes conscious effort, especially if you're not used to putting yourself first. Plan and schedule time for you, set alarms for it, and resist the distractions; this will keep you on track and away from old habits.

How many times do you say yes when you really want to say no? How many times do you undersell your own values to keep others happy or to keep the peace?

In the Bible it says, "But thou shall love thy neighbour as thyself" (Lev. 19:18 KJV). It doesn't say to love our neighbour more than ourselves or less than ourselves; it is saying *as* ourselves, equal and balanced. When you put others before you through obligation and say yes when you really mean no, it's not loving yourself, and it's out of balance. Of course there are times we should help others, but never in detriment to ourselves. You may not realize it, because it's very subtle, but underselling your own values in favour of others through obligation, as well as doing things you don't want to do, triggers soul lessons and old emotional patterns, breeding inner resentment and unhappiness. This leaves you feeling out of balance and frustrated, sometimes for days after, and you may not even realize where this inner frustration is coming from. It's time to start doing more of what makes you happy, which includes living by your own values, staying true to yourself, and learning to say no without fear.

Consciously connected people know they regularly need to stop and give themselves alone time in order to rebalance and go within. They are not afraid to be alone—they relish it.

Wisdom Note: I feel people often get confused with giving. Many of us were taught that it's better to give than to receive. Many of us have also been made to feel guilty for thinking of ourselves; we are taught it is selfish. Even in today's spiritual teachings, such as Mahatma Gandhi and Buddha, they tell us we should focus on the compassion and service to others. I totally agree with this, and our purpose is to love and accept others. I also believe, however, that it should never be in detriment to yourself and your own well-being. If you are out of balance with giving, so much so that your health, finances, and life are affected, what good are you going to be to anyone else? It's all about keeping the balance between yourself and others. Make yourself matter, and then you will be able to give more.

Learn to Be Patient

> Holding out is a superpower. (Danielle Lapore)

Ego is very demanding, but have you noticed that the more you give it, the more it wants? It is never happy. It is always searching for the next emotional high, and when it gets it, it moves onto the next thing. It's the BSO syndrome—bright, shiny object syndrome. You want it, and as soon as you have it, you see the next best thing—and often before you have even enjoyed or finished what you just got.

Consciously connected people have learnt to be patient, because they know that sometimes it takes time to manifest their desires. They have learnt that if they rush in with all bells blazing, they may take the wrong path and end up learning a lesson instead. They patiently wait for their direction to show up, and they always feel within themselves whether or not it is right. If they don't know, they wait. They always sit on BSO decisions until their spirits give them the go-ahead, and they always complete and enjoy each experience fully.

Case Study: Theresa

Theresa had an appointment with me while I was writing this book. The timing seemed perfect to use as a case study. She was confused about her direction. She had started to study coaching and told me it felt right when she signed up, but another opportunity had come up, and now she felt the coaching course was too expensive. Maybe she should be trying this new direction with a multilevel marketing company.

I reflected her to her spirit. What do you really want to do with your life? "Help people like you do, through coaching," she said. Is this new direction going to get you there? "Yes. I will be able to incorporate this into my direction." Incorporate? So it's not directly aligned to your long-term goal of coaching? "No," she said, "but I can still use it as a side business. But I am unsure about the multi-level marketing company." How so? "Because I feel like I could get the same product a lot cheaper, and because it's multi-level marketing, I feel I could be ripping people off." So, does this gel with you? "No," she said firmly. Then there is your answer. Your vibration is saying no—it's not a match. I reminded her that if it's not a vibrational match, she will not make it a success. Regardless of whether her thoughts where right or wrong about the multi-level marketing company being a rip-off, if she felt it was, then that would be her perception and her belief, and therefore she would create this as her reality.

Let's look back at the study course, I suggested. This is what you really want to do, and it will lead you to your goal. Is that right? "Yes," she said, "but it is taking too long, and it's really expensive."

So, let me reflect on what I think you are saying. The study course is the right direction, but the issue is its taking too long, and it's too expensive. "Yes, but probably it's the money issue, really."

Where can you get extra money from? I asked. "I could do two extra jobs a week, and I would have the money. I know I could do this because I have had people walking up to me in the street and asking me to do some work for them."

BSO right there. Can you see it? Theresa was looking for a quick fix to her financial dilemma. It wasn't really about the course, because she needed that for her long-term goal. She was asking the universe, and the universe was giving her opportunity via clients walking up to her in the street with her current job. It was a job that may no longer be her passion, but one she didn't have to outlay any money for because she already had everything she needed. Yet she was giving her consideration and attention to a new direction that wasn't even gelling with her. She would have to start from scratch with the new direction, financially outlay more money, and go and find new customers.

Once the words came out of her own mouth, she could see the BSO in all its glory. She could then stop herself from sabotaging her long-term goal on a BSO that felt new and exciting in the moment but would move her away from her dream and goal.

Did you also pick how her spirit was actually trying to guide her, but she wasn't listening?

1. Her coaching course felt right for her when she originally signed up. Her spirit was saying, "Yes, this is the way to go."
2. The network marketing wasn't gelling with her. Her spirit was saying, "No, don't go this way."
3. Clients were approaching her on the street with money-making opportunities. Her spirit was saying, "Here is the money you need for your long-term goal."

Things are as clear as mud until you unpack them.

Note: This case study in no way reflects my view on multi-level marketing companies. I don't hold a view on this because I believe that they are right for those who believe they are a match for them, and they are wrong for those who don't.

Keep It in the Now

Consciously connected people know that looking back can cause guilt, shame, and frustration—and looking forward can create fear, anxiety, and impatience. They choose to keep their focus on the only moment in time that is real: now. The past is done, and you can't change it, only learn from it. The future hasn't arrived, and your now is going to determine that future. Stay balanced in the now and work on being consciously connected; that will bring the future you want to you.

Step Out of Your Comfort Zone

Consciously connected people understand that the ego is the part of them that wants to keep them in their comfort zones. They know that if they don't step out of it, they will not learn anything and be held back. They feel the fear and do it anyway. When the ego presents with a fear they know they need to overcome, it doesn't stop them. They face that fear head-on and go looking for circumstances to stretch them. If they have a fear of heights, they will jump out of a plane in a tandem skydive. If they have body issues, they will go to a nudist beach and stand naked in all their glory. They will empower themselves by not giving in to their fears and limiting beliefs instead they challenge them.

Wisdom Note: When faced with a really big challenge in life that is bringing up a lot of fear, it's a good exercise to write down everything you think could go wrong. Then find the solution and the blessing for each challenge. Follow it up with everything that could go right. That way you have it covered

Case Study: Kate

Kate was a candle maker who also studied personal training and had started to build a good following with loyal clients. We had been working on soul lessons and emotional filters with her relationship, and she discovered that she and her partner were no longer in alignment. He wanted to start a family, and she didn't want children. He wanted to buy an investment property, and she wanted to spend money on building her business. She had decided that they needed to set each other free to follow their own paths.

Then out of the blue, she made an appointment and showed up having a meltdown. "I can't do it," she said. "How will I survive? I won't be able to pay my bills. What if my business fails?" She was sobbing. "I really want to do this, but I can't."

We had already done the soul lesson work, so I asked Kate, "What is the absolute worst thing that could happen if you take a leap of faith and follow your spirit?"

Kate said, "Well, I could go broke." And then what? "I can't pay my mortgage." And then what? "I would have to sell my house." And then what? "I would have to buy a little, tiny house out in the country and make candles." She started laughing. She felt relieved to find that her biggest issue of not being able to pay her mortgage wasn't really that bad, because she loved making candles too.

Then I asked Kate, "But what if you succeed?" She left with her confidence renewed that she could follow her inspiration and face whatever the outcome was going to be.

Face your fears with solutions and blessings.

Choose Kindness

In every situation, the consciously connected choose to be kind. Even when someone is treating them with disrespect they don't lower their vibration with a reaction of the same type. They respond with kindness because they know that when others treat them with disrespect, it is a reflection of the other people, not them. They know the other people are having ego reactions and have something to learn. Responding with kindness doesn't mean they are a doormat; it just means they stand in their power by not reacting with anger, judgement, and condemnation. They communicate their responses in a loving, firm, balanced, and kind way. This invites the other people to calm down and reflect on their own behaviour, which they would never be able to do while both parties are in reaction.

Keep Your Vibration High

Consciously connected people know that in order to manifest and attract powerfully, they will need a higher vibration and should live life at the level they wish to attract. They do what is required to keep them consciously connected and balanced.

If they want a trustworthy person, they are truthful. If they want to be supported, they support others, if they want to receive abundance, they give abundantly—all in balance and not in detriment to self. In relationships, if they want to attract their ideal partner, they will be the ideal partner they are wishing to attract in.

Get Comfortable with Your Emotions and Feelings

They also understand that it is okay to experience the negative, and they do this graciously. They cry when they need a good cry, they grieve when they need to grieve, they have hissy fits with purpose, they stand in their power, and they stand up for their rights when required. The difference is they don't stay in the negative for too long, and they don't reflect their negative emotions towards others. They own them and use them to evolve and move forward.

Feelings are natural. Feelings connect us to our spirit side of self and let us know if something needs fixing or is right or wrong for us. The consciously connected know that blocked emotional feelings are the way of the ego and its need to protect itself. Consciously connected people are honest people who don't need to hide their emotions for fear of judgement, shame, or guilt because they realise everyone has something to be shameful, guilty, or embarrassed about.

They know the more they hide their shame and guilt, the more power they give to it, and the more it will keep showing up in their lives. They make peace with their past and find forgiveness for themselves for being all they knew how to be at the time. They understand that in the bigger picture, they have nothing to be guilty or shameful about, and that as long as they are evolving out of the old ways, they are moving forward. If you really love yourself, you will forgive yourself, and when you forgive yourself. you will make the changes you know you need to make. People are mostly forgiving by nature; we are more likely to hold a grudge with ourselves than we are with others.

Face it, own it, love it, and release it.

Consciously connected people also understand that blocked emotions need a period of time to unblock, and that one may feel them very intensely when they start to release. They don't allow this to stop them from feeling their emotions by blocking them out again. Instead, they learn how to love them and manage them. You will never rid yourself of your negative feelings and ego, so don't try; simply make peace with your ego and turn your attention to your spirit instead.

Remember that it's okay to feel hurt, angry, fearful, and sad. Give your ego a pet name. I call mine obnoxious Julie, and when she rears her head with a judgement or fear, I tell her to settle down, because we don't do it her way anymore and I own it by looking at what I need to learn.

Wisdom Note: The ego can try to be too saintly as much as it can be problematic. It can be just as emotionally damaging to try to live up to high expectation as it is to dwell in the lower vibrations. We are not here to be perfect; you wouldn't learn anything, and there would be no reason for you to be here. It's tiring to try to live as someone you are not; if you are, then you know what I am saying is true. Make friends with the imperfect part of you, stuff what everyone else thinks of you. Hopefully you have done enough work in this book to realise what judgement really is. You will be so much happier and less stressed if you acknowledge that it's perfectly okay to be perfectly imperfect, just like the rest of us.

Start and End with Good Intention

Consciously connected people start and end their day with good intention. They tell the day how they wish it to be. They program the day with positivity right from the start. If issues arise that they didn't expect, they know that's life, and they may have something to learn. They end their day with inner reflection and intention for the next day to be more positive. The will never let a bad day dictate the next day or their future.

Learn to Communicate

Consciously connected people learn to communicate with others in a way that doesn't cause a reaction with good expression of their feelings and confidence to ask for what they want. They don't assume or presume they ask. If they feel there is a problem, they face it and find out the facts rather than allow their ego to create its own perception. Others are too busy with themselves and their own minds to be reading yours, so never assume someone should know how you feel. If you want something from someone, ask for it with balanced communication.

Here are my three steps for balanced communication.

1. Don't start a conversation with something the other person will perceive as a judgement or blame, or that is likely to push emotional buttons. Keep it general, acknowledge the person, and invite them into the conversation.
2. Express how their behaviour or the problem has made you feel, and how it is affecting your life.
3. Politely tell them what it is that you feel will fix the problem, and what you would like them to do.

Most people are good at steps 1 and 2, but they forget to include step 3. If you do just steps 1 and 2, the person you are communicating with feel the need to defend himself and is more likely to go into justification and defending his actions. By using step 3, you are letting him know what is expected, and so he is not left hanging and wondering what it is you want him to do.

Wisdom Note: Here is a spiritual trick I use when I want to communicate something important to someone that I know may push buttons. I have the conversation with people first on the etheric level in my imagination. I imagine we are having the conversation, they are listening to what I have to say, and there is no conflict. You can connect to someone on the etheric level because we are all connected. If you did it more consciously, you can read others' minds. They will not accept what you are saying on the etheric level if it isn't aligned with their spirits, or if they feel controlled or manipulated, or it's not in their best interest. If your communication is from your higher self and is valid, then you should have a better outcome with the communication when you have it in person. Give it a try.

Never Assume or Presume You Know What's Best for Others

Never assume or presume that people want or need your help and advice. This is a lesson I had to learn. If someone asks me for advice, I will give it. I have had to learn that if people don't ask, they may need to learn something for themselves. We can be there for them, and if they want advice, that's awesome; if not, we can empathetically hold space for them by being there and listening. In the space of listening, they can often work out what they need to do themselves, at the level that is right for them at the time. As carers and leaders, we want to help, and we often know what would help, but it is not always our place to do so.

Case Study: Janelle

Janelle had come straight from the supermarket for her appointment with me. She was a bit frustrated and told me that she had tried to help a lady at the supermarket, but the cashier had rejected her and made her look stupid.

I asked Janelle to tell me why. She told me that a little old lady in front of her was trying to pay for her groceries. The cashier was helping the old lady look through her very empty purse for five dollars to finish paying. Janelle said, "I felt sorry for her. She was clearly a struggling pensioner, and so I offered to pay. I tried to give the cashier the five dollars, but she ignored me and keep looking in the old lady's purse until she found her last five dollars. I thought how mean of her. She made me angry because she should have let me help the old lady."

I asked Janelle if the old lady asked for her help. She said, "No, but she could have used that five dollars. I just know it." I asked Janelle to consider how she would feel if she couldn't pay for her groceries, and a stranger stepped in to pay for her. "Oh, my God, I would be very embarrassed." Do you think the little old lady may have felt the same? Janelle could then see that she may have been robbing this old lady of her dignity, rather than the cashier robbing her of her last five dollars. Janelle also realised she was more ticked off with herself than the cashier.

There Is No Need to Be Offended

We can always find something to be offended about. I usually find it while driving on the M1!

Consciously connected souls know that being offended is keeping them stuck in focusing on the negative, which creates more negative. I believe it was an Esther Hicks talk where I heard it explained like this. God or the universe only knows yes. When you say, "God, I need more money," God says, "Yes, that is right, you need more money." When you say, "God, this person is really getting under my skin," God says, "Yes, that's right, this person really is getting under your skin." When you say, "God, I am feeling happy today," God says, "Yes, that's correct, you are feeling happy today." The law of attraction is only going to say yes to whatever it is you are believing and focusing on. If you're constantly focused on being offended, then being offended is all you will see and all you will be.

Take the opportunity to learn to see things from a higher perspective. I drive a lot from one end of the country to the other, and I have done so for years. I have had a couple of experiences where I have been stuck behind a car, only to later come across an accident that had happened earlier. Could I have been there if I wasn't stuck behind the slower car?

Now, when I get stuck behind a slow driver or someone cuts me off, I try to imagine what the bigger picture may be. I will be honest that sometimes I let out a few swear words first, especially when I have been stuck behind a car that then speeds up in the passing lane so I can't get past. This does my head in, and my ego can't help having a little rant every time—which is probably why I keep attracting it! D'oh!

Forgive

Consciously connected people understand that forgiveness frees them. Some people find it hard to forgive because they feel that by forgiving someone, they are saying, "I acknowledge what you did to me, and I accept that it was okay." This is not the case! You must acknowledge what was done to you, but you do not have to accept that it was okay. It wasn't okay then, and it isn't okay now.

In forgiving people, we acknowledge and accept that they were simply being all they could be at the time they hurt us. Yes, they made negative choices, but they did so armed only with the knowledge they had at the time, and with their own damaged ego and emotional filters created by their soul lessons. Forgiveness does not accept that what they did to you was okay; rather, it understands that there is a big picture. The actions of those who hurt you were reactions programmed from their own past.

I believe that we choose and make soul agreements with our parents and family before we get to the earth plane. You belong to a soul family group in which you have had many lifetimes together. Your lessons here on the earth plane are already programmed into your spirit before you get here, and your childhood from 0-9 years is what forms the basis of this learning. That is why you were born into the family you have, and why all your lessons are linked and mutual. You have already lived many, many lifetimes, and so have your family members and loved ones. You have been hurt, tortured, and probably murdered, and you have also probably hurt, tortured, and murdered others throughout the many cycles of evolution you have undertaken. With each lifetime, you have been given an opportunity to evolve your soul knowledge.

It is no coincidence that family issues run through generation after generation; neither is it a coincidence that soul lessons blueprints and profiles run through generation after generation. Through the process of evolution, you and your soul group family are using each other in the big picture to evolve each member's understanding as a spiritual being. Lifting your energetic vibration into higher levels of consciousness allows you even more access to other realms and infinite knowledge. You are starting to awaken to the essence and truth of who you really are. We all have free will with the freedom of choice, and if we choose not to connect to our soul destiny in this lifetime, that is our choice. If you're unhappy and miserable, then you're not connecting to your truth and the destiny you have chosen.

I believe the mass consciousness on the earth plane right now is, at this very moment, on the tipping edge of this knowledge flowing into the mainstream. The older generations have been forced and controlled by society and the masses in the old ways that didn't support them in their efforts to follow their own direction or connect to their own spirit. No wonder there has been so much pain and so many tortured souls. On the tipping edge is the new way of discovering ourselves by understanding and connecting to the universal laws and our unlimited potential. We are starting to break out of this old mould. We need compassion for the older generations. They were simply acting out of fear and didn't have the knowledge to be able to heal or make the changes like we do today. With our free will and choices, we can either put some effort into changing for the better or continue to repeat the "family" history.

Just because someone has had a tough upbringing or has been through some traumatic events, it doesn't mean these experiences must now control their life. Have a look around you, and you will see inspirational people everywhere who have made the most out of their lives and their challenging beginnings. It is always these people who create more happiness and success than anyone else, because they are empowered by their own evolution and accomplishments. If someone has hurt you, that person is a victim of his or her life and past. Don't allow that person to turn you into a victim too. Rise above the situation and move on.

Think about this: Who is it really hurting when you can't find forgiveness? It is you! Those who have hurt you get on with life because they don't know any better, and because they are blocking their own pain. If they can't feel their own pain, they certainly are not going to be able to feel yours. Set yourself free and take back control of your life by becoming responsible for your future happiness. Hand back to those who have hurt you the responsibility of their own actions and their own evolution, and take responsibility for what this lesson has taught you.

In the big picture, there is a universal law called cause and effect. To everything anyone has caused, there is an effect of the same value. There is no escaping the consequences of our actions in the big picture. I like to use the example of drug dealers. You often see these souls living the high life, driving awesome cars, and living in luxury. From the outside, it looks as if they are getting away without suffering for all the pain they are causing others. Put yourself in their shoes, and you will quickly see their lives are no real party. They are actually living on the edge in their own self-created hell. They live every moment looking over their shoulders, never knowing whom they can trust, never knowing whether someone is going to try to take them out. They never know how much freedom they will have because they live in constant fear of getting caught. People don't need drugs when they are happy and content; people take drugs to escape their own self-imprisoned hell.

You can't escape the universal law of cause and effect; it comes into play every time anyone makes a choice, good or bad. Whatever you give out through a soul vibration and your choices, you will receive back in some form eventually. Think about how it feels when you tell a lie. You might think you got away with it, but your soul vibration knows different. You feel it on the inside with an unsettled feeling. It's not comfortable to tell a lie for most people. That feeling will then attract something of equal value back to you.

Jesus showed us his awareness of a much bigger picture and the ultimate forgiveness when, at his crucifixion, he prayed, "Father, forgive them; for they know not what they do" (Luke 23:34 KJV). They know not what they do. There are a lot of unaware people, and if they understood the bigger picture, I am sure they would consider their choices and the consequences a lot more.

We can't change our behaviour if we are not consciously aware of it. So many people are in reaction to their soul lessons and are not aware of their own behaviour and the pain they are causing. We have the knowledge to change this. You now have a choice and the knowledge to stop any further family lessons and reactions that have been handed down through generations by arming yourself and your children with this wisdom. Teach them love, compassion, and forgiveness so that they can take this forward into the next generation.

Case Study: Tammy

Let me share with you one of my client's experiences. Tammy told me that thieves had jumped her locked back fenced area and stolen her bike. She told me that she needed a more expensive bike because she had outgrown that one anyway, and so she told the insurance company that it was her daughter's bike that had been stolen and claimed more than what it was worth. She then bought the better bike. I asked her what the difference was, and she said about three hundred dollars. I then asked her if there was anywhere she had had to unexpectantly pay out that amount of money. She gasped in horror as she told me she was just about to pay that exact amount of money to fix her car because someone had dented it.

You will never escape your own actions.

> Judge not, and ye shall not be judged: condemn not, and ye shall not be condemned: forgive, and ye shall be forgiven. (Luke 6:37 KJV)

You also need to find your forgiveness for yourself. If you harbour guilt and shame, it's time to love yourself for being all that you could be. No one is perfect. Everyone hurts someone at some time in one's life. Whatever you think you have done, it's time to let it go and give it to God. If it's caused an irreparable situation in your life, find the blessing; it will be there.

We have all done things we are not proud of. Wayne Dyer admitted to having affairs, doing drugs, and drinking too much, before he found his spirit. I too was once unfaithful. I can also look back and think I should have been a much better parent to my kids. I would be able to do so now because I know more now. I am no longer that person back there; I have found my spirit and evolved.

What really matters is that you are moving forward. You are growing and learning that the old you is not you today, and you can continue to change. I accept you for that, and I will not judge you on your past because I know we are all learning and growing; none of us is perfect.

Let's do our review.

I have given you some of the consciously connected wisdom that I have learnt along the way. Of course, there is so much more; I could write a whole book on this subject alone. Again, if you listen to your spirit and your inner nigglings, you will know the areas where you are meant to step up and evolve.

In the next chapter, we are going to look at your soul gifts and your purpose—not that anyone should ever tell you what your purpose is. However, I can give you the energy of your soul gifts to help prompt you in your discovery.

Spiritual Profiling Helped Me Find My Purpose
by Marsha

I remember lying on the floor in foetal position, crying uncontrollably, and feeling utter despair. I was alone, lost, and scared. Suicide crossed my mind. That was fifteen years ago. The pain of my past and my recent divorce caught up with me. It was the first time I'd prayed for days and days, with all my heart. I asked for support, guidance, and direction. What happened next was absolutely a miracle.

I read hundreds of self-help books, and I started to see the light again. My progress was slow—it took ten years. I felt like I'd lived a lifetime and was evolving, but I was exhausted and still suffering from depression.

When another relationship ended, I finally discovered Julie's first book on spiritual profiling, *Soul Lessons to Soul Mate*. I could clearly see how I had also contributed to the relationship's demise. Once I fully understood my life lessons and my master life lesson, I started to feel really excited about the future I had always visualised.

I have been applying the principles and formula from *Soul Lessons to Soul Mate* to my life ever since, including friendships, family, and colleagues. Understanding my own lessons in life has enabled me to respect and understand another person's reactions and characteristics with love, patience, compassion, and empathy. My relationships are blossoming, and my anxiety has gone. I'm now free from the shackles of the past and have forgiven everyone I once held responsible for my situations in life.

With the knowledge I now have from Julie's soul lesson work, I embrace my life lessons with love and kindness instead of explosive reactions, fear, and total despair. And the bonus? It also helped me discover my own life purpose as a leadership development specialist: www.impressyourself.com. au. I can honestly say I am now living a life I love.

CHAPTER 9
The Soul Lesson Gifts

> Your talent is God's gift to you. What you do with it is
> your gift back to God.
> —Leo Buscaglia

When I first wanted to start my own business back in 1991, I had a rubber stamp made. I designed it myself: it was an eye with the Gemini sign as its pupil, and I called it Gemini Visions. I could see myself working as a psychic, helping people and teaching classes. I was so excited when my little rubber stamp finally arrived at the stationery shop.

My dreams where soon crushed when everyone around me said, "You can't do that. People will think you're crazy." Everyone had an opinion in regards to all that could and was sure to go wrong. I tearfully hid that little rubber stamp in the cupboard because I didn't have the confidence or the courage to back myself.

In 1996, I started to slowly build my confidence by doing little readings and even a meditation class with just three people. In 2000, I backed myself even more. I left the safety of my home town, moved interstate, and spent the next few years dabbling with readings, healings, and massage as a part-time pursuit. I set up a room in my home in 2003. It wasn't enough to go full time, so I had to continue with the other ways of earning an income. I am sure I have tried every job possible to find my thing.

I have studied a lot, and I love to research and read. I have a diploma in massage and a diploma in business. I studied sports training and worked as a professional football trainer. I studied fitness and worked as an aerobics instructor. I studied counselling and neurolinguistic programming (NLP) and Cert 1V in training and accessing. I have worked in sales, on a whale-watching boat, as a cleaner, as a masseur, as a trainer in a massage college, and as a receptionist. I have even done some modelling, and work as a makeup artist and photographer's assistant. Although I liked something about all of these jobs, none of them held me for long. I changed every two years on average. My soul was restless and bored, and it wanted to do what it had always wanted to do: help people on the metaphysical level.

After bashing my head for many years while that little rubber stamp rotted in the cupboard, I was on the bare bones of my butt, financially. When you're down to nothing, apparently God is up to something. I finally decided to back myself properly and follow that little voice in my head. I was just about to turn forty, and I had nothing, so I really had nothing to lose. I had to borrow money from my dad, which to me was the most degrading thing I ever had to do in my life. A forty-year-old failure—Dad must have been so proud. I thought if I failed, at least I knew I had given it my best shot.

I finally put my calling into action. I kept telling myself, "These are my gifts, for God's sake, so why wouldn't it work?" It was February 2006 when I finally launched full time as a professional business, and I have never looked back. This is the longest job I have ever had, and it's the one I have loved the most. It wasn't easy back in the early days, if you read my book *The Missing Link* from 2007, you have read how I survived on faith and fish fingers for the first part of my business setup. Now, I am not saying chuck your job in and do it hard, and you will succeed. I am saying that you have your music in you, and if you find out what that is, you will be guided to knowing how you can put your purpose into action. Only your soul lessons and your ego's belief in self will hold you back.

As I mentioned previously, no one should tell you what your purpose is—not even us psychics, who mostly get it right but can also be wrong through interruption. I choose to guide my clients into looking within themselves and use their soul gifts to prompt them.

Your life will be a testimonial to your purpose. Your experiences (both good and bad) and all that you have been learning, loving, and detesting along the way will hold clues. Everything you have done up until today has given you skills. My sales jobs taught me to connect to people. My fitness and training taught me about health. My whale-watching job taught me I wanted freedom in my work. My training and teaching taught me to teach. My training and assessing taught me to write programs. My massage taught me to deal with clients. Modelling taught me to stand in front of people. Your experiences, both good and bad, will also be a testament to your purpose. My book *Soul Lessons to Soul Mate* would never have been written without the experiences I have had through all my own relationships. I have had some people say, "How can you give relationship advice when you have experienced a lot of relationships?" My answer is, "That is what has made me an expert on the topic." It is through my experiences that I have learnt what I now teach. You become an expert on a subject through experience, not a textbook. Your experiences give you understanding; no one knows more than those who have experienced it for themselves.

What is your purpose? Have you ever thought there is something you would love to do or feel you are here to do? If you know, you are one of the lucky ones. If you don't, I want to help you find it. However, you must understand that quite often because of our own belief systems (BS) and soul lessons, we may not believe that this is possible for us at the moment. I didn't when I put my little rubber stamp and dreams into the cupboard. I have heard and used all the excuses: I am too old, I can't afford it, I am too busy. These excuses, justifications, judgements, and blame are simply giving your pain a reason to exist!

There will be evidence throughout your life of your spirit trying to show you what it is you are here to do, especially in your childhood. Children before the age of five will show signs of their true energy. The games they play and the things they love to do will show their hidden talents.

I have the most amazing childhood memory. It's a pity it didn't continue to be as sharp into adulthood. I can even tell my dad what our house looked like inside when I was two. I remember what I loved to do while growing up: I loved teaching my toys. I stole chalk from school (sorry, Tonsley Park Primary School) to write on my blackboard. I always got an A in English. but it wasn't for my spelling or grammar—just ask my editor. It was for my writing and poetry. I was always fascinated by money and business. I walked around the neighbourhood and sold my sisters' baby clothes to all my friends for dolls' clothes. It wasn't a very successful enterprise; I made about a dollar. I could also see spirits from a young age. In the jobs and in the years that followed, I found I most loved the ones where I was helping, leading, and teaching, and where I had freedom.

You can see evidence in all of the above that I have always known what I am here to do. I started off as a psychic, which led me into writing and teaching, and then owning and running my own business.

What draws you in? What jumps out at you as something you love to do? Go back through your memory and ask your younger self, "What did I love to do?" Ask your siblings and parents if you have them around to help you remember, if you can't.

Your spirit will show you if you let it. Even with no memory of the past, you can ask your guides and higher self to show you. What is it you're meant to do? Then see what jumps out at you, what shows up in front of you. You can attract situations, people, and signs to help show you what your purpose is. In order to pick up the answers and the signs, stay in the now, be balanced and consciously connected, and let it present itself to you. Someone may give you an answer. A job may jump out at you and appeal to you. You might read an article. Look for what is showing itself to you and what you are attracted to.

Wisdom Note: Your spirit is always communicating with you. If you don't hear it in your mind or feel it in your feelings, then it will revert to trying to make it jump out at you. You will be attracted to what it is showing you; it will literally stand out. Angels and our spirit families love to help with this as well. They hear you talk to yourself, and therefore the universe, they know what you need help with through your thoughts. So they will try to help make that answer stand out through trying to make the answer grab your attention.

Have you ever had a sign jump out at you that you have never noticed before, but it was exactly what you needed at the time? This is divine intervention and the law of attraction working together. When you are more balanced and consciously connected, you will see this a lot more. You may have heard it called synchronicity or coincidence; it is both, and it's pretty cool, especially when it happens on a regular basis.

Where do you spend your free time? What are doing? If you love doing it, how can you turn it into a career? What job allows you to experience more of this joy?

Not everyone is meant to be a business owner or have a purpose that is grand. Your purpose may be as an everyday hero. I have come across mothers whom I am in awe of. Their purpose is to love children, and they can't get enough of kids—and not just their own. They collect kids from all over the neighbourhood and radiate unconditional love to them. They radiate this love from their inner being, and you know beyond doubt they are fulfilling their purpose. You usually find these mothers with a tribe. When I come across one, I make sure I tell her how special she is, because she is bringing unconditional love to the earth plane and to all these children in a very powerful way.

Your soul purpose is to love and radiate your love into what it is you love to do, including your career and work. Your purpose in life is doing what you love to do.

For every soul lesson, there is also a gift; the law of duality says so. I have included below a list of careers for each number and gift. Use your soul lessons and go through the lists to see if there is anything in your numbers that resonates with you.

If your spirit says yes, but you know from within that it's not possible for you to do so now, then look at the energy of the gift and see if it fits in with something similar. For example, you wanted to be a firefighter, but now you know you wouldn't physically pass the demanding test, and therefore this is no longer an option. Look at the energy of the firefighter. A firefighter is community-orientated service provider who helps and rescues people by putting out fires. Can you do this in another role? Maybe work with your local homeless shelter, or find solutions for the needy. Be a local CFA volunteer. If there is a problem, find the solution.

Sometimes it can take a while, but if you keep asking for the solution, the answer will appear. I couldn't get a name for this book; it just wouldn't come to me. So I asked for it to be shown to me. While I was walking on my favourite mountain, Mount Schank in South Australia, it suddenly popped into my head. I was so scared I would forget it that I sent a text message to myself.

Wisdom Note: The intuitive doesn't come from the intellectual mind, so it can pop in and then pop out just as quick. Intuitive thoughts are harder to remember, and so I have learnt to write them down straight away, or else I lose them. Dreams are the same and come from the subconscious, so write them down straight away, or you risk not being able to remember them.

The spiritual leader Deepak Chopra sums this up like this.

> According to this law [the law of Dharma], you have a unique talent and a unique way of expressing it. There is something that you can do better than anyone else in the whole world—and for every unique talent and unique expression of that talent, there are also unique needs. When these needs are matched with the creative expression of your talent, that is the spark that creates affluence. Expressing your talents to fulfil needs creates unlimited wealth and abundance.

The Soul Lesson Gifts

1. The lesson of independence with the gift of leadership

When #1 profiles step into their authentic selves, they are awesome leaders and healers. They inspire others, and others listen to them. Careers for the #1 include speaker, teacher, coach, manager, entrepreneur, and inventor.

2. *The lesson of codependence with the gift of cooperation*

When #2 profiles step into their authentic selves, they are great organisers and work exceptionally well with others. Careers for the #2 include carer, mediator, adviser, business partner, assistant, tradesperson, human resources, and organizer.

3. *The lesson of self-worth with the gift of expression and creativity*

When #3 profiles step into their authentic selves, they are fantastic communicators and are naturally creative. Careers for the #3 include anything creative, counsellor, artist, singer, speaker, healer, psychic, writer, designer, tradesperson, and inventor.

4. *The lesson of stability with the gift of provision*

When #4 profiles step into their authentic selves, they are a strength to be reckoned with and can be successful in all types of supportive roles. Careers for the #4 include government worker, child carer, carer, accountant, financier, health service provider, tradesperson, builder, office worker, and sports star.

5. *The lesson of control with the gift of choice*

When #5 profiles step into their authentic selves, they can do anything they put their minds to; the world is their oyster. Careers for the #5 include psychic healer, artist, performer, singer, trades, entrepreneur, travel agent, salesperson, pilot, air hostess, and real estate agent.

6. *The lesson of commitment with the gift of community service*

When #6 profiles step into their authentic selves, they are professional and supportive of the big picture. Careers for the #6 include community-orientated support roles such as police officer, philanthropist, firefighter, politician, coordinator, carer, health service provider, and charity worker.

7. The lesson of trust with the gift of teaching

When #7 profiles step into their authentic selves and believe in their pathway, they make excellent teachers and healers. Careers for the #7 include jobs that are creative, psychic, healer, health and well-being professional, and life coach.

8. The lesson of security with the gift of the entrepreneur

When #8 profiles step into their authentic selves, they are the alchemists and can create success in any endeavour they choose. Careers for the #8 are banker, manager, business owner, lawyer, doctor, property, and building developer.

9. The lesson of humility with the gift of the humanitarian

When #9 profiles step into their authentic selves, they change the mass consciousness for the better by bringing attention to humanitarian needs. People, animals, and the environment are what they are here to support. Careers for the #9 are park ranger, charity worker, environmentalist, nurse, carer, veterinarian, philanthropist, and charity worker.

The earth angels 11, 22, 33, and 44 also have the gift of purpose.

If you have a double number in your soul lessons (either 11, 22, 33, or 44), you are what we call an earth angel. An earth angel is someone who has a purpose that will affect and change the lives of others. This can be through directly helping others and making a real difference to the earth plane through their own vibration and gifts, or by bringing about an event that will change the lives of those around them, which then prompts others to make a difference. Of course, people who are not earth angels will also change the lives of others, but an earth angels will have a deep sense of destiny, knowing that they have an extra role to play in the big picture.

You can also be an earth angel through the numbers of your day date of birth, as well as your soul lessons and gifts.

Remember that it can be difficult to connect to your purpose when your soul lessons are getting in the way. The ego that will try to tell you what you can and cannot do. You spirit is always in the background, trying to prompt you and giving you gentle signs and guidance to lead you onto the right pathway.

You are now ready to go within and look deep into yourself. Reading this wisdom should have prompted you in the areas where you can start. It is a journey, and one that will be easier for you if you are balanced. I suggest you read this book often to keep you focused and on track. I know from experience that every time you reread something, you will find more wisdom within the same words, and you will gain a deeper understanding each time you read it. When you evolve, the wisdom will also evolve, and it will be like the onion layers you are uncovering within. You will continue to go deeper and deeper into a higher understanding of wisdom and ultimately yourself each time.

Conclusion

Don't Hide

Don't hide in the shadows, my friend. Come out into the light. Take this wisdom and change your life. You know you can because you were born to do so.

Let me give you a huge hug. You are an inspiration to me and all who walk you path. You are helping to create a heaven here on earth when you make conscious contact with your spirit and shine in your own true light.

The only way to make the world a better place is to bring more love to the physical world, and that starts with me and you.

If you loved this book, then please help me get its message out there. Please share it with your friends, family, and social media groups. You will be helping me fulfil my purpose, and that will on some level also help you fulfil your own. I sincerely thank you.

May love and light and your strong spirit always guide you.

In your honour and with love,
Julie Kay

Afterword

In every moment, you are given an opportunity to choose what you think, say, and do. That is the blessing of free will. Nothing is without consequence, and everything happening to you is happening within you. Therefore you are responsible and in control of changing it. Knowing this inspires us to move forward out of being victims and victimisers and into becoming survivors and thrivers.

It empowers us to take responsibility and make the changes that have repeated behaviours and patterns showing up. It inspires us to listen to our inner spirit and trust more in the guidance we are given every day. It makes us more accepting of ourselves and of others, and that changes the world. If we can all be more accepting and come more from our spirit rather than our egos, then we will live in a wonderful world. I hope you will be part of that vision by making it a reality in your own life now. If you do, this will be your experience because your outer world will reflect your inner world. You will be creating your own heaven right here on earth.

Special Offers

If you have found you need help identifying your soul lessons and what you are learning, as I mentioned in chapter 6, I am offering a special price to help you. Go to www.juliekayinternational.com and click on the contacts page for more information.

If you would like to learn so much more and put this learning into practise straight away, then you may love to join Julie at The Shift Sanctuary. This is a three-day, four-night, live-in, intensive training in a beautiful natural retreat in Northern NSW. There's a limit of eight people per training because it is very deep work. We aim to keep this training as affordable as possible to be accessible to everyone. Just mention the code JSSLLL8 for $100 off your training. A full deposit is still required. Visit the website www.juliekayinternational.com for more information on The Shift Sanctuary.

Author Bio

Julie Kay describes herself as a light crusader and self-empowerment activist. Julie has worked professionally for over two decades as a psychic medium and spiritual profiler, and she has been teaching metaphysical wisdom for over twelve years. In an age where personal fulfilment and a greater ownership of our own happiness are sought, Julie's sole purpose has been to empower herself and others in expanding this awareness of self-understanding and accountability through consciously connecting to our own inner world and spirit.

As a naturally enthusiastic entrepreneur with a humanitarian heart, Julie is also an inspiring author. She has also published *The Missing Link* (2007), *Soul Lessons to Soul Mate* (2013), and *Life after Life Communication, 3rd Edition* (2015). Julie has written and facilitated over twenty intuitive and spiritual development workshops, including the highly regarded three-day, live-in Shift Sanctuary Program in northern NSW, a program that launched in 2013 as the Love Life Retreats and has already changed the lives of many in a profound and lasting way.

When Julie is not travelling for personal appointments and workshops, she can be found on the beautiful Gold Coast in Australia. A devotee of sun, sand, and surf, Julie loves to come home to Queensland to relax and reconnect to her loving family and fabulous friends.

Julie can be contacted at:

E-mail: info@juliekayinternational.com
Web: www.juliekayinternational.com
Facebook: Julie Kay Love Life Community Page